JERRY POTTS
PALADIN OF THE PLAINS
B.D. FARDY

MR. PAPERBACK®

P.O. BOX 3399, LANGLEY, B.C. V3A 4R7

A Sunfire publication. Its trademark, consisting of the words "Mr. Paperback" and the portrayal of a lion, is Registered at the Canadian Trademark Office, Hull, Quebec.

JERRY POTTS—Paladin Of The Plains

PRINTING HISTORY
First printing—June 1984

Canadian Cataloguing in Publication Data

Canadian Cataloguing in Publication Data

Fardy, Bernard D., 1949–
    Jerry Potts, Paladin of the Plains

ISBN 0-919531-18-0

    1. Potts, Jerry, 1840?–1896. 2. North West
Mounted Police (Canada) – Biography. 3 Metis –
Northwest, Canadian – Biography.* I. Title.
FC3216.3.P6F3 1984 971.2'02'0924 C84-091501-2
F1060.9.P6F3 1984

Contents

PRODUCTION CREDITS

Editor—T.W. Paterson
Cover artist—C.W. Jeffries (drawing); Garnet Basque (colors).
Maps—B.D. Fardy
Design & Layout—Garnet Basque
Typesetting—Kirkrod Printing Ltd.
Printing—Hignell Printing Ltd.

PHOTO CREDITS

Montana Historical Society: pgs. 13, 18, 25, 39, 58, 67 (bottom), 86, 92, & 128.
Glenbow-Alberta Institute: pgs. 31, 36, 63, 67 (top, left & right), 71, 83, 96, 100, 105, 110, 114, 116, 119, 122, 140 & back cover.
Public Archives of Canada: pgs. 42, 45, 52, 102, 127, 133, 134 & 136.
Saskatchewan Archives: pg. 56.
Canadian Cattleman: pg. 61.
Royal Canadian Mounted Police: pg. 7, 88, 95 & 99.

CHAPTER ONE

The Early Years

HE has been described as the greatest scout and guide of the old west, one without equal on either the Canadian or American plains. Although accurate, this description does not entirely depict a man who was one of the most important and colorful characters of the Canadian northwest during its infancy of settlement in the last decades of the 19th century. His skills and achievements should rank him with those more famous but probably less accomplished heroes of the American western frontier such as the Kit Carsons, Wild Bill Hickoks and Buffalo Bills.

Yet he is not as famous as most of his contemporaries. Kit Carson led expeditions through the uncharted wilderness of Nevada and California, but he never did it in a blinding blizzard. This man did. Wild Bill Hickok could pull his six-gun and shoot the center out of a silver dollar thrown in the air, but he never trimmed his moustache with bullets. This man did. Buffalo Bill had a Wild West show filled with "wild" Indians like Sitting Bull, but he never knew the great Sioux chief when he was really wild. This man did.

He is truly one of the unsung heroes of the old west—a "Renaissance man" of his time and place. He was equally at home in the composed council teepees of the Blackfoot Indians or the whisky soaked, scurrilous saloons of the whiteman's frontier towns. He could track like a bloodhound, ride like a Cossack, fight like an Indian, swear like a trooper, shoot like a hired gunslinger, and drink like the proverbial fish. He was in reality one of those independent, laconic, and disturbingly mysterious men of the all too often stereotyped hero of a western novel or Hollywood movie. He was the classic loner.

All the tired cliches apply. Some should have been coined after him. He was strong, and not only in the physical sense, yet he had his weaknesses. He was habitually silent, yet on rare and auspicious occasions eloquently loquacious. He was gentle yet savage, brave but never foolhardy, loyal, yet to some seemingly vacillating. Always a gentleman, he was often a rogue, and by the Victorian standards of his day he was considered immoral, yet in the worldly ways of his Indian ancestry he was deeply religious. The man, like his life, was the quintessential paradox.

While he sometimes behaved in a manner that was not favorably looked upon by effete easterners of his day, he also evinced an integrity and loyalty that many of his would-be detractors did not know the meaning of and a courage and resourcefulness that they were not capable of. When this strange, insoluble solution was stirred in the boiling cauldron that was the Canadian northwest of the late 1800s, and mixed with the white and red blood of the two races he was born of, it poured out as a Metis man—Jerry Potts.

Potts' story began south of the U.S.-Canada border in 1836. That year his father, Andrew R. Potts, a Scotsman recently arrived from his homeland, got a job as a clerk with the American Fur Company at their most northern post, Fort McKenzie, on the upper Missouri River in what would later be known as Montana Territory. Andrew Potts had become an employee of the Company by way of Pennsylvania where he had lived for a short while after emigrating from Scotland. He was a learned man from a successful family and had at one time studied medicine. There is some suspicion that an indiscretion in this field prompted him to flee his homeland and seek obscurity in America. If such was the case he certainly accomplished his objective by ending up in Fort McKenzie, which at that time was the last outpost of civilization in the American northwest.

This post had been founded in 1832 by trapper David Mitchell and named after his boss Kenneth McKenzie who was the owner of the Upper Missouri Outfit, the American Fur Company's most important northern subdivision. McKenzie, another hardy, rawboned Scot, was known as the "King of the Missouri," ruling over the headwaters of the mighty river that was described as "a little too thick for a beverage and a little too thin for cultivation."

Shortly after the establishment of the trading post McKenzie succeeded in getting promises of peace from the Indians of the area. The country around the headwaters of the Missouri marked the territorial boundaries of the Blackfoot, Cree, Crow Assiniboine, Sioux and Gros Ventres. The Indians kept their treaty with the whites as far as the fort was concerned but gave no assurances about peace among themselves. When Andrew Potts arrived there in 1836 he found it to be very dangerous country.

Although the traders had an agreement with the Indians, lone white hunters looking for beaver pelts and other furs found themselves favored targets of the Indians, especially the Blackfoot. In the first year that the fort operated the Blackfoot killed 57 white trappers.

Soon after his arrival at Fort McKenzie, Andrew Potts took a young Blackfoot girl, "Namo-pisi" or Crooked Back, of the Black Elks band of the Bloods, to be his wife. A year or so later they had their first child and named him Jeremiah. The name, like the man it belonged to, was not an imposing one; but before long young Jerry as he would be called, would be affectionately known as "Old Jerry," and his reputation would spread far and wide as a man you could ride the river with as a friend or a man you should stay clear of as an enemy.

Jerry Potts was not much more than two years old when the violent world he was born into touched him personally. In 1840 he was initiated into the bloodshed and brutality of a way of life that would span another 40 years. One summer day in that year his father was busy handing out trade goods through the barred wickets of the fort when a surly Piegan named "Ah-pah," or One-Eye, got into an argument with a French Canadian "engage" named Marcereau. One-Eye may have demanded more for his furs or made some remark about Marcereau's Snake or Shoshoni wife, but whatever the cause of the altercation Marcereau threw the belligerent Piegan out of the fort on his ear. "Ah-pah" nursed his bruised ego and planned his revenge.

Later that evening One-Eye skulked back to the fort and lurked in the shadows as dusk became night. It was Marcereau's job each evening to lock the wooden shutters on the barred wickets and tonight when he did so the Piegan planned to see to it that it would be his last time. Inside the post Marcereau's boss sent him on another chore and told Andrew Potts to lock the fort up for the night. When Potts' face appeared in the bars of a wicket One-Eye fired his trade musket point blank into his face and shot him dead.

The Piegans had liked and respected their white brother in trade and when they learned what had happened they promptly closed "Ah-pah's" other eye—permanently. If little Jerry Potts had been able he probably would have thanked his half-brothers, for One-

Eye's wanton act of vengeance caused him to be thrust into what were probably the most ignoble years of his life.

Left without a husband, "Namo-pisi" was on her own. During this period of initial contact between the whites and the Blackfoot the Indians proudly followed their traditional ways, confident that they could at any time wipe out the few traders at Fort McKenzie. Sqaws who became the wives of whitemen were not readily reaccepted into the teepees of their tribe. Left to her own resources, Crooked Back had to survive the best she could.

At Fort McKenzie at this time was one Alexander Harvey, a man with a somewhat distasteful reputation and, it is said, a proclivity for Indian women. Andrew Potts' young wife caught his eye and he made her his "woman," reluctantly accepting her young child as his "son." Harvey had come to Fort McKenzie in 1833 with Prince Maximilian and the afterwards famous artist Carl Bodmer on their expedition to the upper Missouri in 1833-1834. A saddler by trade, Harvey was from St. Louis where some inclination or indiscretion prodded him to seek a more secluded life in the northwest. In 1830 he went to work for the American Fur Company post at Fort Union as a hunter.

Harvey was a big man, standing about six feet tall and weighing 200 pounds. He had great endurance and strength, cared for nothing or no one and was said to be without fear. Prince Maximilian whom Harvey had accompanied up the Missouri, said that he was able to pick up the whole carcass of an elk and carry it off on his shoulders.

Harvey was indeed a charmer. On one occasion when a Blackfoot stole a pig from the fort he pursued the Indian and shot him in the leg. He strolled up to the wounded man, passed him a pipe and invited him to have a smoke. As the cringing, suffering Blackfoot accepted the pipe, Harvey began talking to him about how fine a day it was and what a beautiful country they lived in. He then told the Indian to take one last look around and coolly shot the man's brains out.

By 1841 command of Fort McKenzie had been handed over to a man named Francis A. Chadron, who succeeded Alexander Culbertson. Chadron was another character of questionable virtue and he and Harvey got along famously. But Harvey's antics and wicked demeanor finally strained even the tolerance of the rough and ready men he associated with, so much so that they complained to the head office in St. Louis. When Pierre Chouteau, owner of the American Fur Company, summoned him to St. Louis to answer for his outrageous conduct, Harvey left Fort McKenzie with winter approaching; he travelled all the way down the Missouri in a canoe with nothing more than his rifle and dog.

Chouteau was so impressed by this feat that he granted the trapper a plenary indulgence and sent him back upriver the following spring. With Harvey went a trapper named Charles Larpenteur, to whom Harvey bragged, "I never forgive or forget." When they reached the upper Missouri posts of Clarke, Union and McKenzie, Harvey sought out the men who had tried to get rid of him and severely beat all of them. One of these, a Spaniard named Isodore Sandoval, became an implacable enemy of Harvey.

Some time later, when Harvey and Sandoval were sent downriver with a load of furs to Fort Pierre, everyone laid even money that only one of them would return. To everyone's surprise both did. Back at Fort Union, Sandoval began to parade around the post with his rifle, loudly boasting that he was going to kill Harvey. Knowing that he was drunk, Harvey stayed out of the Spaniard's way.

The next day all of the clerks and engages were ordered to begin preparing an order of goods for Fort McKenzie and when Sandoval did not show up Harvey and Culbertson, the manager of the post, went to look for him. They found him in a sutler's store and, smarting from the previous day, Harvey asked him what he had meant by all his loud talk. Sobered, Sandoval tried to ignore Harvey, but the strapping saddler challenged him outside to fight. Leaving the sutler's Harvey strode outside and waited for the Spaniard to come out. When Sandoval did not appear the trapper strutted back inside and said, "You won't fight me like a man so take this!" Lifting his rifle Harvey shot the Spaniard in the head. He then invited any of Sandoval's friends to take up for him but none would.

That autumn Harvey returned to Fort McKenzie and during the winter Chadron's negro slave was murdered by a party of Indians. Bent on revenge, Chadron enlisted the aid of his old friend Harvey to help him in his plan. The factor said that he believed that the Blackfoot had killed his slave and in the spring when they returned to begin trading he would blow the hell out of them. His plan was to conceal a cannon among the trade goods and massacre the Indians as they rode in. All he needed was a gunner. Harvey agreed to be his triggerman. Chadron induced Harvey with the promise that once all the Indians were dead they would claim all the horses, furs and guns as recompense for his murdered slave.

When spring arrived it was no matter that the first party of Indians to arrive at the fort were not the ones responsible for the killing. Chadron meant to have his revenge and any party of redskins would do. But their plan only partially worked, owing to the suspicion of the Blackfoot. When Harvey touched off the cannon he fired into a smaller party than he had hoped for. Only three Indians were killed and three more wounded. One of these was the chief of the band and as he lay injured Harvey sauntered up to him and finished him with his knife. He then ordered the cowering and defenseless squaws to do a scalp dance around their dead and dying brothers and husbands. For all their scheming and savagery Harvey and Chadron got little booty.

The result of their devious attack had long lasting effects. The Blackfoot became hostile and their incessant attacks throughout the summer forced the traders to abandon Fort McKenzie and move down river to the mouth of the Judith River where they established Fort Chadron. The Blackfoot burned Fort McKenzie to the ground and its ruins afterwards became known as Fort Brule and its site simply Brule, or burnt, Bottoms.

Within another two years those who wanted to get rid of Harvey decided to do it themselves, and this time they would do it for good. His depredations had become so vile that they decided to murder him. They devised a plan to trap and kill him, but when he physically fought his way out of it against overwhelming odds, they allowed him to leave the country.

Harvey left the upper Missouri in 1845 and made his way to Fort Pierre where he found a gang of American Fur Company malcontents who banded together with him to form the Harvey-Primeau Company. Their company offered stiff competition to the American Fur Company for many years and Harvey attained a degree of the power and riches he had craved his entire life. Alexander Harvey was either one of the most skillful men on the upper Missouri or one of the luckiest.

In 1845 Jerry Potts was about seven years old and again without a "father." Had he been capable he would have recognized the fact that he was much better off.

The next year the American Fur Company again established a trading post in Brule Bottoms. Honest men had worked hard to undo the damage Harvey had done in 1843 and had succeeded to the extent that a new trading post was possible. It would be a long time before the Blackfoot would completely trust the whites again, but they realized that they needed the whiteman's trade goods if they were to remain as strong as their enemies. The new fort, named Fort Lewis, soon came to be known as Fort Benton.

To this newest fort came the newest manager of the American Fur Company's frontier posts. An educated and gentle man, Andrew Dawson was another Scotsman who soon earned himself the sobriquet, "last king of the Missouri." After Harvey's departure from the northwest Jerry Potts had remained with the traders as an orphan ward, moving with the men from post to post. Dawson, in his gentle way, "adopted" the orphan and cared for him as if he were his own son. As Potts grew through boyhood the kindly Scotsman taught him all the values he had not learned from Harvey.

It is not clear where Potts' mother was at this time, but Crooked Back had probably returned to her people very soon after she realized just how evil a man was Harvey. Under Dawson's patient and instructive care Potts received a semblance of education and, more importantly, learned the ins and outs of the fur trading business and the ways of the frontier. He became well-versed in the ways of both the white and redman. In his travels with his foster father he learned to speak several Indian languages which included, besides his native Blackfoot, Cree, Sioux and Crow.

By 1850 Potts had rejoined his mother's people in southern Alberta, just north of the U.S.-Canadian border. He spent the next several years among the Blackfoot learning their ways and showing that he was very much an Indian. As he lived and travelled with the Bloods he became proficient with bow and arrow and a crack shot with a rifle. He also became an excellent tracker and honed to perfection what in later years would prove to be an almost supernatural sense of direction.

While with the Bloods he ranged through the huge expanse of plains that was the Blackfoot domain. Bounded on the north by the North Saskatchewan River, on the south by the Missouri, on the east by the Cypress Hills and on the west by the Rocky Mountains, it was the best buffalo range in the northwest and home of the great northern herd. Potts travelled the country extensively on the yearly buffalo hunts and soon knew every mile of it. He also mingled with and learned the ways of his Piegan and Blackfoot brothers.

As he grew into manhood Potts became very religious in the Blackfoot ways and steadfastly loyal to their customs and traditions, sharing their superstitions about the power of dreams and medicine. On a visit to Fort Benton he had a dream one night in which he was told that a cat living in the post could protect him from evil. Waking, he went and searched every corner of the post until he found the cat sleeping in the early sun. Killing it, he immediately skinned it and after tanning the hide wore it around his neck as his "medicine" for the rest of his life. His loyalty to his Indian blood was a virtue that would mark his involvement with the Blackfoot throughout his life. Although he belonged to two races his first allegiance was to the Indians and he would always show a preference for their way of life.

When he reached his late teens Potts moved frequently between the camps of the Bloods and the American Fur Company post at Fort Benton. Although preferring the life of the Indians, he was also loyal to his foster father and ever grateful to him. During these frequent excursions to Benton, Potts discovered that there were some ways of the whiteman also worthy of attention and he enthusiastically adopted many of the raucous and carefree ways of the unbridled frontier. Between the sedated, sagacious council teepees of the Blackfoot and the raw, wild trading posts of the whites, Potts learned the best and worst of both worlds.

At Fort Benton he was schooled in the rough and ready ways of the lawless frontier, soon acquiring both the skills and the vices of the frontiersmen. He grew fond of gambling and downright religious about drinking. He also became very skilful with a revolver. Often he would demonstrate his expertise with a Colt, showing all the coolness and marksmanship of a gunslinger (usually when he was drinking).

His favorite exhibition was executed with a partner, another mixed blood by the name of George Star whom he met at Fort Benton. The two Metis were kindred spirits and remained longtime friends; for Potts it was one of the very few real friendships he made in his lifetime. Whenever they got together at Fort Benton they would renew their friendship with a game of cards and a bottle of red-eye. After well fortifying themselves with rotgut they would saunter into the street and face each other at 20 paces. Pulling their pistols they would take aim in turn and try to "trim each other's moustache" with lead. They performed this "trick" many times and despite their always inebriated condition neither man was ever touched by a bullet. Potts knew it was simply good shooting but his Blackfoot brothers believed he had supernatural powers which they attributed to his "medicine."

If Potts had any real weakness in his inscrutable character it was his shameless love of the "pure." Like most men of his day he preferred refined spirits but, if they were in short supply, then he was just as fond of the traders' firewater. In fact, he was fond of anything that contained alcohol and had a kick to it—anything as long as it could "blow your hat into the creek." When he was particularly thirsty, he would guzzle Jamaica ginger, essence of lemon or Perry Davis' Painkiller. In desperately dry times he was even known to drink a palatable potion compounded by a Boston firm for a common female complaint.

By 1860 Potts was working for his foster father and the American Fur Company. Dawson sent him to Fort Galpin, an obscure

Fort Benton, Montana circa 1868. At the headwaters of the Missouri River Fort Benton was the terminus of the riverboats that carried supplies to the American northwest. By this time the rough, frontier town was the mercantile center for all the trade carried on with the northern Blackfoot on the U.S.-Canadian border.

company outpost some miles from Fort Benton where his skills were applied to hunting and interpreting.

Potts was then 23 years old and to look at him he was not a very imposing figure. He stood about five feet six inches in his moccasins on stubby, bowed legs that had been moulded around the belly of a horse. His rounded, sloping shoulders always gave him the appearance of standing with a slouch. A straight-nosed, angular face stretched tight with swarthy, bronzed skin was punctuated with piercing black eyes that told little of the thoughts behind them. A black, drooping moustache framed his tight-lipped mouth. Dressed in a fringed buckskin jacket of the frontiersman and the leggings and moccasins of the Blackfoot, his shell belt hung with a sheathed scalping knife and beaded parfleche.

He was a laconic, almost taciturn young man and his manner and appearance probably caused him to be discounted by many. One day at Galpin however, a French Canadian named Antoine Primeau learned that the unimposing Potts was not to be fooled with.

Unfortunately, Primeau learned too late. As a result of a drunken quarrel the two men stepped out into the street to settle their differences. Potts shot Primeau dead.

The gunfight was obviously a man-to-man duel and Potts was neither arrested nor dismissed from the American Fur Company for the killing. The incident established his reputation as a fighter among the rough frontiersmen of the upper Missouri country and few men would rile him, especially when he was drinking. During the next couple of years Potts stayed in the employ of the American Fur Company and continued to add to his reputation for pluck and toughness.

In the spring of 1863 the annual supply of trade goods for Fort Benton had to be left 400 miles downriver at Fort Union because the water levels in the Missouri were too low to allow the paddlewheelers to proceed any farther north. Outside of Blackfoot country, where there was only a tenuous peace at best, there was open warfare. This was the time of the great Sioux wars and Red Cloud and his warriors were trying to wipe out the white presence in their territory. They were having tremendous successes along what had become known as the Bloody Bozeman Trail in Wyoming and southern Montana and wanted to do as well in the upper Missouri country.

But Dawson needed his supplies if he was to have a successful year of trading with the Blackfoot. The job would be a dangerous one and he decided to fetch the freight himself. He chose the best of his employees to accompany him. His chief clerk Matt Carroll would go with him: two brothers, Jim and Bob Lemon, a man named Joe Cobell, and, to guide and scout for them, his foster son Jerry Potts. The party would have to move the goods upriver by wagon through 400 miles of country infested with thousands of hostile Sioux.

The trip down the Missouri to Fort Union was made without incident. There the supplies were loaded aboard the wagons and the train moved out for Fort Benton on the morning of October 23, 1863. Three days later as the wagons slowly rounded a bend in the Missouri called Ash Point, Potts, who was scouting ahead, spotted a large band of Indians headed in their direction. His keen eyes quickly picked out the trappings that marked them as Sioux and therefore trouble.

He gave the signal to have the wagons drawn into a circle and Dawson quickly had the men follow the scout's direction. The Sioux war party pulled up out of rifle range and milled about discussing their plan of attack. The whites checked their weapons and waited. Finally, one of the Indians, a big, powerful looking man, rode out of the ranks of his companions and slowly approached the wagons. Using sign language he explained that he came in peace and wanted to talk with the leader of the whitemen, shake hands with him and smoke the pipe.

Dawson's men were suspicious. Matt Carroll had spent many years in Montana territory, most of them among the Sioux and he knew these Indians better than any of the other men. He explained that the Sioux had been on the warpath against all whites for the past three or four years and that Red Cloud was determined not to cease hostilities until he had won his war.

Carroll's warnings convinced the men that the warrior's peaceful platitudes were not sincere. Some of them then called for fighting the Indians but Dawson reminded them that it was the policy of the American Fur Company to try and gain the trade of all tribes, including the hostile ones.

Reluctantly accepting Dawson's decision, Matt Carroll agreed to meet the Sioux warrior, but not as the Indian expected. Sure that the Indian was planning some treachery Carroll prepared for it. Before leaving the protection of the wagon circle he took his pistol from his holster and tucked it into his belt behind his back. Carrying his rifle, he stepped over a wagon tongue and started across the prairie towards the lone Indian. The Sioux dismounted and laid down his rifle. Carroll put down his also and the two met about halfway between their lines. As they met the band of Sioux began to shuffle forward slowly.

The Sioux warrior was indeed planning treachery. He had hidden a scalping knife beneath his buckskin shirt and as he took Carroll's hand he began to pull the knife with his other intending to stab the whiteman in the back. He froze stiff, his eyes going wide with terror when Carroll shoved the cocked six-gun into his surprised face.

"Now, dog," Carroll said, "you are shaking hands with a whiteman. Go! Tell your people that a whiteman gave you your life—that the palefaces know how to kill and how to spare their enemies. Go now, and ask your medicine men if they cannot send a better warrior to meet a whiteman."

The band of Sioux began to move forward as their champion began his retreat. Carroll called out to the warrior telling him that if the others came any closer he would be the first to die. The shaken warrior signalled his friends to halt. Carroll withdrew to the safety of the wagons and the Sioux, accepting their leader's defeat, retired without attacking.

Potts rode out to make sure they had moved on. Certain that they had, he returned to the wagon train and Dawson had it formed up and they continued on to Fort Benton without further incident. Potts learned a valuable lesson from the confrontation between Matt Carroll and the Sioux warrior. It and other incidents would help to make him in later years probably the best diplomat in the Canadian northwest when it came to dealing with Indians. He would become a master at it and his intuitive perception would help defuse many potentially explosive situations.

CHAPTER TWO

The American Fur Company

W HEN Lewis and Clark returned from their expedition to the American northwest in 1806, they brought back stories of the riches to be made from furs in the vast, empty land. Far up north in the Canadian country the powerful Hudson's Bay Company were undisputed masters of the trade, had already established themselves on the Pacific coast, and were steadily pushing towards the great plains from across the Rocky Mountains.

The news brought back by the pair of American explorers started a stampede of adventurers and entrepreneurs from the Louisianna country and the east who all wanted to get a piece of the lucrative business. By 1810 several small companies and dozens of free trappers were operating on the lower Missouri and pushing ever deeper into the plains country of the northwest. One of them, John Jacob Astor, dared to follow in the very footsteps of Lewis and Clark and, by 1811, had established his fur trading capital of Astoria on the Columbia River in Oregon Territory to compete with the Hudson's Bay Company on the Pacific coast.

Within a few years, however, Astoria floundered and Astor retired to New York where he invested his huge profits in real estate. Others rushed in to fill the gap. Chief among these was the Rocky Mountain Fur Company founded by trappers and mountain men of the west, and the Columbia Fur Company made up of enterprising easterners. By the mid 1820s the fur business was again so lucrative that Astor decided to have another go at it.

He returned to St. Louis and established the American Fur

KENNETT MCKENZIE

Called "King of the Missouri" by the rough and ready mountain men of the American northwest, Kennett McKenzie ran the American Fur Company with the fist of a tyrant and the tastes of a dandy.

Company; using his large reserves of capital, he soon bought out all the smaller firms operating in the lower Missouri River country. By 1827 he had rid himself of his most northern competition by buying out the Columbia Fur Company.

Some of the men who ran the small companies absorbed by Astor were experienced and capable managers and the fur king made two of them junior partners in his new company. He then sent them into the upper Missouri country to capture the as yet untapped wealth in that region. He could not have picked two better lieutenants than Pierre Chouteau and Kenneth McKenzie. Chouteau was ruthless and unscrupulous and not above resorting to gunplay to have his way. McKenzie, while more affable and genial, was no less determined.

Astor ordered Chouteau and McKenzie to seize the western fur trade at any cost and by any means, hoping to expand his monopoly of the east to include the west. They were to "ecraser toute opposition." And smash the opposition they did. In 1829 McKenzie established Fort Union on the Missouri, making it the most northern post in Indian territory. From there McKenzie expanded into the country to the west, cajoling or threatening the free traders into joining his company. Two years later he established Fort McKenzie at the "three forks" of the Missouri, the most northerly point of navigation on the river.

Now there only remained the Rocky Mountain Fur Company to deal with. Astor backed McKenzie with all the money he needed and soon he was buying furs for nine dollars a plew and selling them in St. Louis for half that. The small independent operators of the Rocky Mountain Fur Company could not long stand up to competition like that, McKenzie thought.

It was not long before McKenzie had earned himself the title "King of the Missouri" and he lived up to it. At his headquarters in Fort Union he lived in the lap of luxury, eating the best food, drinking quality wines and brandies, and smoking fine cigars. He dressed his Indian mistresses in the latest styles from St. Louis and reigned supreme on the upper Missouri. He was tough, shrewd and ambitious. Once, when told that an Indian attack on a band of his trappers had resulted in the men escaping but all of their horses being captured, he ranted that it should have been the other way around.

For all his power and backing, however, McKenzie found that the Rocky Mountain Fur Company was not as easy to put under as he had thought. Made up of old, grizzled mountain men like Jim Bridger, Joe Meek, Bill Sublette and James Beckwourth, they stubbornly resisted his efforts to put them out of business. Although

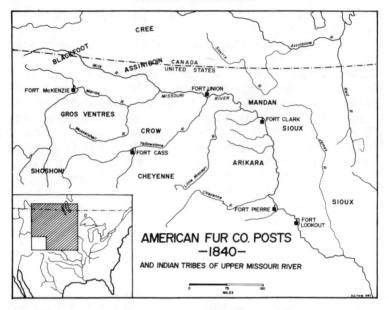

AMERICAN FUR CO. POSTS
—1840—
AND INDIAN TRIBES OF UPPER MISSOURI RIVER

he steadily gained ground each year, McKenzie met his downfall before the Rocky Mountain Fur Company.

When the trappers and mountain men of the small company gathered for their rendezvous on the Yellowstone River in 1833, they were surprised to be met there by the "King of the Missouri" himself. McKenzie gave them a royal reception fitting of his importance. He treated his competitors to roast beef and mutton, milk and cheese, bacon and butter and spoiled them with his fine wines and cigars. He also made comely Assiniboine maidens available.

But he got a little carried away with his generosity and also offered them moonshine from his private still at Fort Union. Whisky in Indian territory had been forbidden by an act of congress earlier that year; there was a political uproar and Astor was publicly embarrassed. The "King" was dismissed from the Company the next year and retired to private business in St. Louis.

That same year, however, he saw the Rocky Mountain Fur Company finally succumb to the pressures of his former employers. Astor had his monopoly but it was to be a short-lived empire that he ruled over. The Company had a rather languid existence over the next 10 years as fur hats were slowly going out of style. By 1843 the Oregon Trail opened up the previously inaccessible country of the northwest to settlers.

The American Fur Company stayed in business for another 20 years when at last it, too, had to give way to the changing times. Just as it had pushed the trappers and mountain men into oblivion it was in its turn pressed into the pages of history by the undeniable tide of settlement.

In 1864 the American Fur Company went out of business after 40 years of operation and its demise gave birth to the new age of the "free traders." This meant that anyone who had the capital and the courage could trade competitively with the Indians of the northwest. But the era of the fur trade had all but run its course and a new commodity caught the interest of the traders: The industrialized east was looking for thick, tough leather that could be used to drive the machinery belts of progress. The hides of domestic cattle were too thin and wore too quickly. Out on the sage covered plains of the west there was a beast whose dried hide was found to be as tough as iron. However, before most whitemen on the frontier could be interested in the trade in buffalo hides there were other, faster and greater fortunes to be made.

That year gold was discovered in the Alder Gulch region of southwestern Montana. Hundreds of hardened and near poverty-stricken men who had made their livings with the fur companies caught the fever and flocked to the area. Not even the threat of Red Cloud's warriors could deter them from seeking their fortunes in the rugged and dangerous country.

A man named George Steele, unemployed as one of Andrew Dawson's chief clerks at Fort Benton, decided to seek his fortune in the ore pockets of Alder Gulch. He interested a young tenderfoot in his prospecting venture, then began looking for a guide to take him into the unfamiliar country of the Sun and Smith river areas. Jerry Potts was also unemployed and Steele, knowing well the competence and skills of the young scout from their days together at Fort Benton, asked him if he would guide his small expedition. Potts agreed.

Potts had known Steele for some years and knew his reputation. The Indians called the ex-clerk "Sleeping Thunder" because of a volatile nature which lay hidden beneath a calm facade. Steele later joined the U.S. Army, became a colonel and went on from there to become Indian Agent for the Blackfoot in Montana.

Steele outfitted his tiny party at Fort Benton then hit the trail. The trio spent several weeks prospecting along the Sun River and, after finding nothing, decided to head back home across Red Cloud's country. They were only a few miles out of Fort Benton and just beginning to relax their vigilance when suddenly, out of a coulee, charged almost 200 screaming Sioux warriors. The three prospectors wheeled their horses and whipped them into a full gallop.

As they rode the men shouted back and forth to one another about what they should do. Their horses were tired after the long trek and the fresher Indian ponies were gaining on them. Potts had noticed a deserted log cabin about two miles back in the coulee and said they should try to make it back there. Under cover, he said, they would have a better chance of making a stand. There was only one slight difficulty with Potts' strategy: The Sioux were between them and the cabin.

In a daring move Potts suddenly reined up as they rounded a bend in the trail and yelled to the others to follow him. Wheeling their horses the three charged back into the oncoming horde of Sioux. The plan seemed a little foolhardy but Potts was counting on the element of surprise to make the dash through the Sioux lines safely. With no time to argue Steele and the tenderfoot followed his lead. As the Sioux rounded the bend they were met by the charging whites, their guns blazing. The surprise Potts had counted on, worked. The three raced through the startled, scattering Sioux and reached the log cabin.

Jumping from their horses Potts instructed them to quickly unsaddle. The entrance to the old soddy was too low to allow the horses to enter so the animals were turned loose. The door to the cabin was off its hinges and Potts quickly turned it on its side across the entrance and braced it with logs from the fireplace so it could serve as a barricade.

When the howling—and smarting—Sioux arrived on the scene they slid from their ponies and began to move in on the cabin on foot. Well-directed rifle fire from the defenders' repeaters turned them back before they could reach it. When Potts' rifle was empty he pulled his six-gun and demonstrated his deadly skill with the weapon by dropping six Indians with six shots.

Realizing their strategy was costing them too much, the Sioux withdrew to devise an alternate plan for the kill. Potts knew they would wait for dark to burn the whites into the open. By dusk, he had his own plan thought out. Grabbing his saddle blanket and tossing aside his hat, he slinked out of the cabin. Stealing through the brush he made his way about a quarter of a mile around the Sioux camp to its rear. Wrapping the blanket around his shoulders he ambled down into the Indian camp.

His knowledge of Sioux allowed him to pass unchallenged

through the camp until he found the horse herd unguarded and hidden from the flickering light of the fires. In the rope corral he picked out three fleet looking ponies and slipped off their picket lines. Quietly, he led the horses back to the cabin and signalled Steele and the tenderfoot to join him.

Saddling up, the men slipped down the coulee and up the slope to the prairie above. As they topped the rise, something primitive in Potts urged him to call out his triumph to the unsuspecting Sioux below and he let out a blood-curdling Blackfoot warcry, informing his enemies that this time he was the victor in the age-old sport of war.

Once back in Benton, Potts allowed that his fur trading and prospecting days were over. He settled down with the Piegans in their camp on the Marias River, about 50 miles northwest of Benton. There was little work for him as a hunter or scout since the American Fur Company had folded and he was not much interested in the gold that so many whitemen went crazy over. Then, too, there was the more practical side of his reasoning: The country south of the Missouri was just too full of Sioux.

On the Marias, Potts returned to the Indian way of life. He was earnest about settling down, for shortly after he took himself a wife. The first Mrs. Potts was an 18-year-old girl named Mary from the Crow tribe. Although her people and the Blackfoot were longstanding enemies, Potts showed the paradoxical nature of the Indian who would make a friend or take a wife from a tribe that he traditionally treated as an enemy.

During the next several years of life among the Piegans, Potts earned a reputation as a warrior among the tribes of the Blackfoot Confederacy. One winter's morning he left camp, crossed the frozen Missouri and rode into Benton where he tended to some business. Leaving town, he headed south along Shonkin Creek to hunt buffalo for his camp. While riding along the creek he was suddenly confronted by seven Crow braves. Three of the Indians were armed with bows but the others carried awkward but lethal breech-loading trade rifles. Potts' marking identified him as Blackfoot but in his laconic way he offered no greeting, even though he knew the Crow language and was improving on it through his wife.

Confident because of their numbers, the Crows used sign language to explain to their harmless looking guest that they had a large camp on a creek a few miles from the Shonkin and that they would like him to visit their chief. Realizing that he had no choice Potts agreed to go with them. The three with the bows headed out and Potts fell in behind them while the four riflemen followed him.

As they rode along the Indians behind Potts began to discuss what they should do with the little half-breed Blackfoot. A couple of them wanted to take him to their chief but the others were in favor of taking his scalp now. After a little haggling they decided that Potts' scalp would make a better trophy than his carcass. Unaware that Potts was warned they rode on a little longer.

When Potts heard the cold metallic click of a rifle being cocked behind him, he moved. He tumbled from his horse just as the bullet went whistling over his head. Rolling in the snow the metis came up on his knees, levering his repeating rifle. Before the surprised Indians could control their spooked horses or bring their heavy rifles into play, Potts triggered off a fusilade of shots that dropped all four into tangled heaps of bodies and horses and spraying snow. Wheeling on the three bowmen, he found them desperately quirting their horses through the impeding snow.

Catching his horse, Potts mounted and headed back to Benton. On his way through that morning he had seen that there was a large party of Piegans as well as some Bloods camped in the town. Upon returning he went to his Piegan and Blood brothers and told them of his encounter with the Crows. Within an hour he was leading a large, anxious war party of Blackfoot towards the unsuspecting Crow camp near Shonkin Creek.

Night was coming on when they reached the enemy camp. The Blackfoot quietly surrounded the Crows in the quickening dusk and struck suddenly in the last twilight. The surprised Crows could do nothing but try to escape. As they desperately tried to flee the Blackfoot killed dozens of them and left many more wounded in the camp. Flushed with victory, the Bloods and Piegans finished off the wounded, lifted scalps and rode back to Benton for a victory celebration.

At the trading post the triumphant Blackfoot went wild. They held a great scalp dance in the streets of the town celebrating with singing, dancing and general hell-raising. The revelry continued long into the night and the terrified citizens of the town locked themselves in their houses and root cellars, fearful that the Indians would go completely crazy and wipe them out. It was probably due to the influence of Potts and other Metis among the party that the Blackfoot were restrained from tearing Benton to pieces.

It was incidents like these that earned Potts the Indian name of "Bear Child." The appellation was an old and honored one among the Blackfoot and Potts carried it proudly throughout his lifetime. Although it had not been given to him because of his prowess in battle it could have been.

Fort Benton in the early 1870s had become a bustling frontier town, the gateway to the sprawling Northwest.

Some months after he led the attack on the Crow camp on Shonkin Creek, he and a younger cousin were hunting near Sun River when they were ambushed by three Crows. Their first shot dropped Potts' cousin with a fatal chest wound. Jumping from his horse, Potts scrambled into some brush for cover. While waiting for the Crows to move in on him he heard them a little way off discussing their plan of attack.

Again Potts' knowledge of the Crow language saved his life. The Crows decided to use deceit to try and capture their second scalp of the day. They would tell the Metis that they were satisfied with one scalp and that he was free to go. As he rode away they would shoot him in the back.

Gesturing in sign language they relayed their message to Potts, telling him that he was to leave his rifle behind. Once he agreed, Potts knew the advantage would be his as he would have surprise on his side. Laying down his rifle Potts remembered an old trick Matt Carroll had taught him and tucked his six-gun into his belt under his shirt. The Crows watched him as he crawled from his cover and walked to his horse and mounted. As he began to walk his horse away two of the Indians ran to his dead cousin and began to strip him as the third kept his rifle trained on Potts.

Potts had gone only a few yards when he heard the sound he was waiting for. At the clicking of the rifle hammer he ducked in the saddle, kicked his feet free from the stirrups and tumbled to the ground. As he fell he heard the bullet whistle by; upon hitting the ground, he rolled and came up on his knees with the Colt in his fist. He shot the Crow with the rifle before the Indian had time to react. The other two started to flee but Potts killed them both on the run.

Packing up his cousin's body, Potts stripped the dead Crows of all their valuables. One of the items he took was the rifle with which the Indian had tried to kill him; he would keep it the rest of his life as a war trophy.

A year or so later, Potts and a group of Piegans were camped on Two Medicine River when they were attacked by a mixed party of Assiniboines and Gros Ventres. The Indians struck at dusk but, despite the element of surprise, the Blackfoot defended themselves well. Only minutes after the fight began they had turned the tide against their enemies. One of the main reasons was Potts. When the attackers struck, Potts grabbed his rifle and dashed to a high point of land where his repeater did deadly work. It is not known exactly how many of the Assiniboines and Gros Ventres he killed that evening, but the toll was enough to raise his status as a warrior among the Blackfoot to a much higher plateau.

His earned reputation as a warrior during these years among the Piegans and Bloods won Potts the highest respect and deepest trust of his full-blood brothers. Soon he was being asked to sit in on tribal councils where his advice and opinions on matters were of importance to the bands. Before long he became a sub-chief among the Piegans and had his own small band of eight or nine lodges on the Marias River.

Although, during these years, Potts' life-style was more that of an Indian than that of a whiteman, he never completely succumbed to the Blackfoot way of life. He would take no part in attacking enemy camps for scalps, nor would he instigate a fight with them. But if the band he lived with were attacked or if he heard of an attack on a Blackfoot camp nearby, he would willingly and ably join in the fight. Neither would he take part in raids for horses or booty. His upbringing among the traders had taught him the whiteman's concept of private property and the law. He had learned that, in the whiteman's world, a man had to work to acquire property and theft of it brought harsh punishment. He had also learned that property bought or traded for by one man could not be claimed by another seeking recompense or revenge for some other theft.

While Potts appeared to shun white society in favor of the teepees of the Blackfoot an incident in the late 1860s showed that he indeed believed in the ethic of private property and did not hold with stealing, whether the thief was white or red.

A Fort Benton man named W.S. Stocking bought a grey horse for $150 and took it to his ranch, where it was stolen that night. Upon making inquiries, the rancher learned that the horse had been stolen by a Piegan and both the grey and the Indian were in Potts' camp on the Marias. A few days later Potts was in Benton and Stocking explained the situation to him. After hearing the stockman out, Potts agreed to help him get his horse back.

Next morning the two men left town and rode to Potts' camp. During the day Potts wandered around the camp, discreetly asking questions. Returning to his teepee, he told Stocking that he had located the horse and was satisfied that it belonged to him. In his cool, deliberate way he invited Stocking into his lodge for a supper of boiled "boss ribs," or buffalo hump, and after eating sent for the Indian who "owned" the horse.

When the Piegan arrived Potts asked him where he had acquired the grey horse. The man claimed that he had bought it from another Indian. Following Potts' diplomacy, Stocking offered to buy the horse for a reasonable sum. The Piegan then presented a long list of goods, ranging from cartridges for himself to calico for his wife. His outrageous demands came to about $500 and Stocking said that he could not pay that much. When the Indian left, Potts told the rancher that he was more certain than ever that the Piegan had stolen the horse. His exorbitant demands had been made, he said, to ensure that he would not be proved the thief. Stocking realized that there was little he could do. He could not risk calling the Indian a liar and knew that in the Indian way Potts could not either. When the Metis invited him to share the hospitality of his teepee for the night the rancher accepted.

Just before dawn the next morning, Potts slipped from his lodge and made his way to the horse herd. Picking out the grey he led it back to his teepee. He then awakened Stocking and told him to take his horse home. "Jerry was about the most decent specimen that I ever met with," Stocking later said of the Metis, "certainly a remarkable man, one with the sinews of a panther and the heart of a lion."

In 1869 Potts' wife Mary bore them their first child whom they named Mitchell. Perhaps feeling a little more responsible, or maybe just tiring of the sedentary life of the past several years, he decided to go to work again. There was little work to be had in the Fort Benton area, but up north the "free traders" were pushing deeper and deeper into almost virgin country that was destined to be known as "Whoop-Up" country.

CHAPTER THREE

The Kainai—Potts' People

THE Kainai, along with the Sitsika and Piegan were an Algonkian tribe that made up the powerful confederacy known as the Blackfoot nation. In their own language they called themselves the "Nitsi-tapi," or Real People. They are believed to have migrated from the eastern forests in the early 1700s as the vanguard of the Algonkian tribes and finally settled on the southwestern plains of Canada in the foothills of the Rocky Mountains.

When they arrived on the plains, according to their own traditions, the tribe separated into three groups to guard their newly acquired territory. A visitor to their camp asked to speak to their chief and everyone claimed to be the head of the tribe. The visitor called them "Akainai," the tribe of many chiefs, and the name was adopted by the tribe. It was left to the whites to call them Bloods.

On the plains between the Bow River of Alberta and the Sweetgrass Hills of Montana, they followed the nomadic life of buffalo hunters and numbered about 4,500 before the coming of the whites in 1800. They lived in small camps made up of extended domestic families each with its nominal leader and making up the larger bands which comprised the sub-tribe. They had a communal life-style and little sense of private property. After acquiring horses from the south and guns from the north they grew very powerful and warlike and were soon feared by all the tribes around them. Their raiding and warring traditions were more often than not the cause of hostilities between themselves and the whites.

Their whole way of life depended on the buffalo and they hunted it by different methods depending on the country they found themselves in. When cliffs were available the Bloods used the jump, driving the animals over the bluffs and finishing them off below with spears and arrows. Another method used was the surround, the men of the band stalking the herd on foot and shooting the best animals while the others milled about. The third, and for horsemen such as they, favored method was the run which pitted horse, rider and arrow against the running buffalo.

Deeply religious, the Bloods worshipped the sun, moon, stars and the powers of the animals. From these things they took their "medicine." An Indian's medicine was carried in his medicine bag and contained the sacred objects which gave him his power or "magic." Their rituals and ceremonies were attended by sacred prayers and great feasting and dancing, and smoking of the pipe which to the Indians was not a sign of peace but rather a deeply religious gesture whereby they acknowledged the presence of the Great Spirit and asked his blessing for the occasion at hand.

Their greatest celebration was the annual Sun Dance, held each summer. The whole tribe would gather for a long session of feasting and dancing, the main purpose of which was to prove and confirm the courage and strength of the tribe's warriors. A sacred Sun Dance lodge was built and in it the braves of the tribe would show their courage and endurance by self-inflicted torture on themselves. Some would cut slits in the flesh of their chests and suspend themselves from ropes tied to the poles of the lodge, then dance to the entrancing beat of drums until they pulled themselves free of the ropes. Others would pull a heavy buffalo skull strung from their backs or be tied to a horse and dragged.

Among the Bloods, said by many to be the most warlike of the Blackfoot tribes, warring and raiding was considered to be an honorable way to earn respect and fame. Their raids for scalps and horses were attended by great ceremony, all of the participants turning out in their finest regalia for a preparatory dance.

War honors were ranked in order of importance. The highest honor was given to a man who wrested a gun from an enemy and bloodlessly counted a coup. Closely behind ranked the taking of a medicine shield or bow or war bonnet. Next came the taking of a scalp, and lastly the stealing of a horse.

The Bloods followed this way of life for more than 100 years before it was interrupted by the coming of the whiteman. By the 1870s they had been decimated by several outbreaks of smallpox and other diseases, and whisky and guns had left the once proud

One of the most important rituals of the Blood way of life was the annual performance of the sacred Sun Dance. Each year the tribe would gather as the young braves would inflict self-torture to prove their courage and manhood and attain status as a warrior.

and near invincible nation of Blackfoot a race of vagabonds in their own lands. In 1877 they gave up their lands in a treaty to the Canadian government and accepted reserves where, although they did not perish as a people, they ceased to exist as a free Indian nation.

Whoop-Up country lay across the Canadian border in the southern part of what would later be known as Alberta. With the demise of the American Fur Company the "free traders" pushed monumental change onto the northwestern plains, the greatest effect of it being felt by the Blackfoot Indians. Small, independent traders competed with the larger, more solvent firms for the trade of the Indians, which by the end of the 1860s was almost exclusively for buffalo hides. The domain of the Blackfoot was also the range of the huge northern buffalo herd. Lacking the capital and scruples of the bigger firms, the "free traders" traded with the cheapest commodities they could find. One of the cheapest was guns but the cheapest thing, and the item Indians craved most, was firewater—pure, rotgut whisky.

By then most of the Indians in northern Montana and southern Alberta were armed with Henry and Winchester repeating rifles. Fortified with firewater they made unrelenting and merciless war on one another. The situation was so bad by 1868 that the U.S. Army was compelled to move into the area in violation of their recent treaty with Red Cloud's Sioux, in an attempt to stop the illegal trade in guns and whisky and the intertribal warfare. That year they established a military post in Fort Benton on the site of the old American Fur Company trading post. Within a year or so they had significantly curtailed the traffic in guns and whisky to the Indians and calmed the country down considerably. But they had no jurisdiction above the boundary line, in Prince Rupert's Land. The whisky traders simply moved north.

The traders saw the vast plains of Alberta, populated only by buffalo and Blackfoot, as a huge gold mine which, instead of being scattered with nuggets of ore, was piled high with the hides of buffalo. According to the frontier standards of the times, these traders were decent men for the most part. In their own minds they did not believe that they were doing anything that was particularly harmful, either socially or morally. Most of them believed that they were trying to make a living in one of the few ways available and that they could not be doing all that much wrong if civilized and enlightened men in far away towns and cities were competing with and encouraging them. But they were all tough and tried men and did not hesitate to use their guns when the situation demanded it.

They came first in wagons, parking on the open plains and waiting for the Indians to come to them. They traded their wares over an open tailgate but soon found that a drunken Indian refused more whisky became very dangerous, even deadly. In these early days more than one trader was found dead beside his looted wagon. In 1869 the traders began to build "forts."

The first one to go up was at the strategic confluence of the Belly and St. Mary's rivers. It was built by two Montanans, John Healy and A.B. Hamilton, the nephew of one I.G. Baker who funded and owned the trading post and operated out of Fort Benton. A semi-circle of crude log huts connected by a flimsy picket fence, the "fort" was not much of an improvement over the tailgate of a wagon. Miffed Blackfoot braves burned the "fort" to the ground soon after it was opened.

Not men to be put off so easily, Healy and Hamilton rebuilt it. This time they did a proper job. The fort was rebuilt of heavy rectangular logs with two bastions on diagonal corners covered with earth roofs and each armed with a brass cannon. The walls were set with

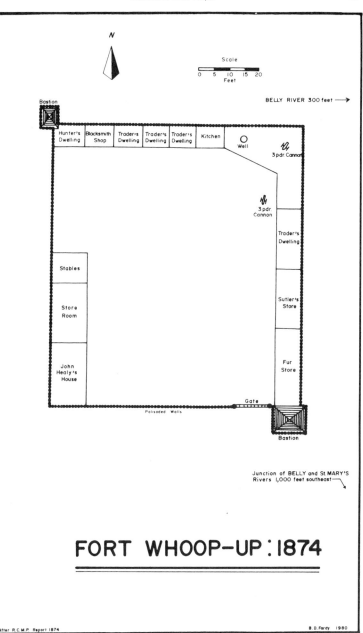

FORT WHOOP-UP : 1874

loopholes for firing through and there was a heavy wooden gate. To the right of the gate were three barred wickets through which the trading was done. The interior was more like a hotel than a frontier post, with spacious rooms and high fireplaces. It had a blacksmith shop, cookhouse, storehouses and living quarters. It took 30 men several months to complete under the direction of a master carpenter who had plied his trade for years with the Hudson's Bay Company. Fort Hamilton, as it was named, was the cream of the whisky "forts."

Through the barred wickets of the fort, John Healy, who took charge of the post after Hamilton returned to Benton, went about the business of his employers at the I.G. Baker Company. Healy was a strapping, six-foot Irishman with a reputation for being somewhat of a hellcat. A Fenian sympathizer, he lived up to his name and during his time in the country was the indisputable king of the Canadian northwest. His political persuasions were definately and vociferously anti-British as his Fenian affiliations suggested, and he was not the least bit shy about it—even in her Majesty's Dominion. Above his frontier fortress he flew his own homespun version of the Stars and Stripes.

Such an ambitious and illustrious a fort as Whoop-Up, as Fort Hamilton came to be known, needed the services of an accomplished and competent guide and hunter. Healy and his cohorts knew that they were in dangerous country and dealing with Indians they knew very little about. To survive they would need the skills of a man who knew the ropes, the country and the Blackfoot. Jerry Potts' reputation was known far and wide in the northwest by this time and he was approached by the I.G. Baker Company about acting as hunter and interpreter for their outpost at the edge of the world. Potts agreed to go to work for them and in 1869 he headed north for the Whoop-Up country.

His wife did not want to move so far away from her people so when Potts left for the border he went alone. Mary returned to her tribe. In the pragmatic Indian way, Potts married again, but this time instead of taking just one wife he took two. He bargained with a Piegan chief named "Sitting-in-the-Middle" for the hands of his daughters "Panther Woman" and "Spotted Killer" and took them both into Canada with him.

At Fort Whoop-Up Potts was kept busy supplying fresh meat for the 30 or more men who manned the bulwark of the traders thrust into the last stronghold of the Blackfoot. Daily, he watched the Indians come to the fort with their piles of buffalo hides and shove them through the wickets for the trade goods. In exchange for their buffalo hides the Blackfoot received tobacco, salt, sugar, flour, tea, axes, knives, blankets, calico and trinkets such as wire, beads, and silver ornaments. They also received repeating rifles and whisky. These last two were to prove a deadly combination.

Although Potts had a great taste for the firewater himself, it was only now that he began to see the destruction it was having on his people. He soon realized that it was not the trade goods that the whites were interested in trading for the buffalo hides. Despite their ignorance of the whiteman's ways the Indians demanded an equal exchange for their hides when the traders offered them food and provisions. But when whisky was available the Indians would offer a pile of hides for just one bottle of the traders' poison.

This vile concoction was a foul and often fatal brew that the traders passed off as whisky. The staple recipe called for quart of watered whisky, a pound of chewing tobacco, a handful of red pepper, a bottle of Jamaica ginger, and either a quart of blackstrap molasses or red ink to give the desired color for either rum or whisky. The brew was then heated to make it potent. The impact this poison had on the Indians was horrendous.

During trading, the Indians were not allowed inside the fort. They pushed and shoved at the wickets eagerly shoving their hides through the bars and greedily grabbing the rifles and firewater. The latter made them go crazy. Drunken quarrels and savage fights would break out among them, many ending in death. Whole camps would erupt into drunken orgies of violence with friends and brothers turning on one another. Men would sell their wives and sisters for a cupful of the fiery brew. Those driven out of their senses by it would try to scale the walls of the fort where they would be pushed off by long poles kept handy for just such a purpose. Even the chimney had to be barred for the most desperate of the Indians were known to slide down it in an attempt to get inside the fort.

In the fall of 1869 a Piegan Indian from the south brought the dreaded smallpox to the Blackfoot of the Canadian plains. As the Indians began to fall sick the old ones among the tribe recognized the terrible plague that had wiped out almost two-thirds of the Blackfoot confederacy in 1837. They knew that the tribe was just as helpless now as it had been 30 years before. By winter the epidemic was at its peak. The Indians panicked and tried to flee the scourge as if it were an evil spirit borne on the wind.

Whole bands were caught on the trackless plains and perished in savage blizzards. In the camps, relatives watched loved ones swell up like bloated carcasses, the stench of their sickness filling the teepees. Others looked on as the afflicted became disfigured or

(Above) The most famous of the whisky forts, Whoop-Up was also the strongest and the most successful. It was run by American traders who considered the Canadian northwest a no-man's land and they were not the least bit hesitant about flying their homespun version of the Stars and Stripes over Her Majesty's soil.

(Below) Many of the so-called whisky "forts" in the Canadian northwest were actually no more than a trader's cabin like the one seen here, from which the trader plied his wares of whisky, guns and, in some cases, legitimate goods. Pictured here is Fort Stand-Off, at the junction of the Belly and Waterton rivers.

went into a raving delirium from which there was no recovery. Young braves killed themselves rather than face disfigurement. Fathers killed their wives and children then themselves to avoid the agony of the disease.

Sometimes whole camps went crazy, recklessly attacking their enemies in a form of mass suicide. Others attacked Fort Whoop-Up and tried to give the plague back to the whites whom they believed had caused it, by rubbing their sores on the gates, doors and window bars. They even stacked their dead to the windward of the fort hoping that the air would carry the disease to the whites barricaded inside.

By spring the plague had run its course and the Blackfoot regrouped to count their losses. The Piegans alone had lost 1,000, while the Bloods and Blackfoot had about 600 dead each. The mighty Blackfoot confederacy, although not completely destroyed, was decimated. What the whiteman's guns and whisky had failed to do in seven years, disease had done in seven months. At Fort Whoop-Up Jerry Potts saw and understood. In its first year of operation the fort had grossed more than $50,000.

Other traders, hearing of the success of Fort Hamilton, moved into the Whoop-Up country and established more forts. Whisky traders flooded into southern Alberta and built posts along the main rivers at crossings that the buffalo-hunting Blackfoot frequented. At the confluence of the Belly and Waterton rivers they erected Fort Stand-Off, later called Fort Kipp after the half-blood who had founded it. Fort Spitzee, a corruption of the Blackfoot word "ipitsi," meaning high, was established on High River. Fort Slide-Out, built by a group of Fort Benton men, was given its peculiar name when the men heard that the post was going to be attacked and decided that they had better "slide out" while they were still able. There were others: Elbow River post at the junction of the Bow and Elbow rivers, French's post at Blackfoot Crossing (the later site of Calgary), and Robber's Roost post.

These forts were run by tough and reckless men, most of whom did not give a damn about the country or the Indians. Elbow River post was run by a crony of John Healy named Fred "Slippery" Kanouse who was a noted killer and a self-styled medicine man who claimed to have a cure for the "pox." Spitzee was operated by a man called "Liver-Eating" Johnson, a grizzled old mountain man better known south of the border as the Crow Killer. He had a long running blood feud with the Crow Indians and was said to have killed more than 20 of them. His cannibalistic sobriquet came from the tale that he had once cut the still-quivering liver from one of his victims and eaten it raw. Such were the men that went to the Blackfoot as emissaries of white civilization.

Spitzee, unlike the other forts in Whoop-Up country, was not a trading post. It was the field headquarters of a growing company of wolfers, men who sought the skins of the prairie canines rather than the buffalo to capture a share of the dollars from Fort Benton and St. Louis. Although they had no trading contacts with the Indians they had plenty of others—all hostile. The wolfers did not shoot their prey because bullet holes spoiled the pelts. Instead they killed large stands of buffalo and poisoned the carcasses with strychnine. The wolves would eat the poisoned meat and be picked up at the wolfers' leisure. The trouble was the dogs from the Blackfoot camps ate the poisoned meat too and hundreds of them died. The Indians resented the way the wolfers wasted their precious buffalo and were outright enraged at the way their dogs were being killed. Any wolfer that came into the sights of a Blackfoot Winchester was as fair game as any buffalo that came into the sights of a wolfer's rifle.

The wolfers were led by two hardcases, John "Chief" Evans and Harry "Kamouse" Taylor, who protested to the traders about selling guns and ammunition to the Blackfoot. Those guns and bullets, they claimed, were used more often on them than they were on the buffalo. Their protests fell on deaf ears. The traders despised the wolfers almost as much as the Blackfoot did. Evans and Taylor then decided to exterminate all the traders in Whoop-Up country.

They formed what they haughtily called the Spitzee Cavalry and, gathering their ranks, thought they would strike right at the heart of the matter by destroying Fort Whoop-Up first. Jerry Potts was busy with his chores at the fort one day in the early summer of 1870 when he and everyone else were alerted that a large group of heavily-armed wolfers was riding in. Healy told his men to be ready for trouble and gathered them around as he sat down outside his headquarters beside an open keg of gunpowder to receive his uninvited guests.

The Spitzee Cavalry rode into the fort and crowded the traders menacingly. Evans demanded that Healy stop trading guns to the Blackfoot and stick to whisky or else he and his men would take every trading post in the Whoop-Up country apart, piece by piece.

Healy was not easily intimidated. Taking the lighted stub of a cigar from his mouth he held it over the open keg of gunpowder. Then he told Evans that if he and his men did not get the hell out of his post right then he would blow the fort to bits, along with everyone in it. Knowing the Irishman's reputation, Evans retreated as gracefully as possible. The Spitzee Cavalry did not stop until it

Manager of Fort Hamilton, John Healy ran the Spitzee Cavalry out of Whoop-up country, then was himself run out by the Mounties. Later a sheriff in Montana, he refused to co-operate with the Mounties when they requested his assistance.

had reached Fort Benton and they never bothered Healy or his trading posts again.

As the summer passed and the trading continued, Potts became more and more aware of the harm that the whiteman's firewater was having on the Blackfoot. As dangerous as the country was for traders and wolfers, Potts still moved among the camps of the Blackfoot in safety. His allegiance to the Indians was never in doubt and they knew that their half-brother had no direct part in the debauchery the whisky traders were spreading among their tribe. His reputation was firmly established among the Blackfoot as a warrior and chief and if there were any doubts about his loyalty they were dispelled in the autumn of 1870.

During the summer the hereditary enemies of the Blackfoot, the Assiniboines and Crees, learned that the Blackfoot had been devastated by smallpox the winter before. Believing that the Blackfoot were no longer strong enough to defend their hunting territory they grew brave and decided to move into Blackfoot range for the fall buffalo hunt. Led by Cree chiefs Piapot and Big Bear, and Assiniboine chief Little Mountain, a hunting party of about 800 braves crossed the South Saskatchewan River in September and moved deep into Blackfoot country.

They camped on the Little Bow River and sent scouts out to locate any Blackfoot camps in the area. When scouts found a small encampment of Bloods in the Oldman River valley, the Crees and Assiniboines thought they would hand their old enemies another defeat. What the scouts had failed to notice was a trail leading to the south where a large band of well-armed Piegans were camped after having fled across the U.S. border following a tragic massacre at the hands of the U.S. Army on the Marias River.

Four years earlier the Crees and Blackfoot had fought a savage engagement on the Battle River far to the north in which the outnumbered Blackfoot had routed the Crees. Still smarting from that defeat, the Crees planned to take their revenge. The Blood camp on the Oldman River was made up mostly of old men and women and children who were out gathering firewood. The Crees and Assiniboines fell on it with a fury and slaughtered everyone except a fleet-footed 13-year-old boy who carried the news to his Piegan cousins. The Piegans, still stewing over their fight with the U.S. Army, grabbed their Winchesters and ponies and headed for the Oldman River.

On their way north they had to pass Fort Kipp and, hearing that Potts was there on some business, rode in to ask him to head up the war party. They found their war leader with his old friend George

Star, partaking of some of the trader's better quality redeye. In his marginally sober state Potts eagerly consented to lead the war party; if the Crees had known his reputation as well as the Blackfoot they probably would have fled if they had known he was coming.

Potts asked Star if he would like to come along and the half-blood cheerfully agreed. It was a vengeance-seeking party of Indians that Potts led out of Fort Kipp on the evening of October 23, 1870. The head trader at the post, Howell Harris accompanied the party as an observer and left an eyewitness account of the last great Indian battle to be fought on the Canadian plains.

The Piegans rode all night to reach the Cree-Assiniboine camp on the Oldman River. Arriving there in the early morning hours, they quietly surrounded it. At dawn Potts gave the signal to attack. When the Crees and Assiniboines poured out of their teepees, they were met by a hail of bullets. In complete disorder, the Blackfoot enemies retreated across the plains until they reached the banks of the Oldman River. There, they took cover in the deep coulee that ran down from the prairie to the water.

Potts led the Piegans into another coulee that ran parallel to that occupied by the Crees and Assiniboines. The two forces were completely hidden from one another by a ridge that ran between the two coulees which varied in width from 20 to 200 feet. From the coulees the Indians crawled up the sides of the ridge to snipe at one another with rifles and arrows and to hurl rocks down on each other. This stalemate continued for a couple of hours when Potts discovered the trump that would give his force the winning hand.

The Metis spotted a small butte to the rear of the Cree-Assiniboine lines which gave a commanding view of their position. Picking the best rifle shots, he sent them to the butte to pour a withering fire down into the enemy ranks. From their secure position the small party of Piegan riflemen began to take a heavy toll of the Crees and Assiniboines.

Realizing that they had little chance if they stayed where they were, Piapot and Big Bear gave the order to run. En masse, the Crees and Assiniboines broke from the coulee and headed for the river and the prairie beyond. When they emerged Potts was ready for them. He led the Piegans in an all-out charge. Caught between the two Blackfoot forces the enemy scattered into the river. As they struggled to cross the deep water the Blackfoot lined up on the riverbank and slaughtered them by the dozens.

In the final charge that drove the Crees and Assiniboines into the river, Potts was at the forefront. As he charged into the melee a retreating Cree suddenly wheeled, levelled his rifle at Potts' face

Piapot, Cree Chief (standing front, second from right) was one of the Cree chiefs who fought Potts and the Blackfoot on the Oldman River in the fall of 1870.

and fired almost point-blank. At the last instant Potts threw himself to one side as the gun roared in his ear. Hitting the ground he lay stunned for a minute, then jumped to his feet and rejoined the fight. But it was almost over, at least on this side of the river.

As the last of the Crees and Assiniboines were being finished off by Blackfoot war clubs and scalping knives, Potts prepared to cross the river and join in the pursuit of those that had managed to swim the river. Just then an arrow smacked into his leg and he went down.

Across the river the Piegans were hot on the tails of the fleeing Crees and Assiniboines, killing more as they scattered across the plains. One group of about 50 Crees tried to make a stand in a clump of trees. They were wiped out to the man. Scores more were killed before the Piegans finally broke off the attack. Of the 800 Crees and Assiniboines that had invaded Blackfoot territory, more than 300 did not leave. Among the casualties was Piapot. Although he escaped with his life, he carried a Blackfoot bullet home with him in his leg. For the rest of his life he walked with a limp.

Back on the banks of the Oldman, Potts and the Piegans took stock of their wounds and casualties. The Blackfoot had lost 40 dead with dozens more wounded. Beside the arrow in his leg, Potts found that the left side of his face and ear had severe powder burns from the rifle shot that had almost blown his head off. He knew he had been very lucky, but the Piegans attributed it to his medicine and the incident only served to deepen their belief that he had supernatural powers and could not be touched by a bullet.

Of the battle itself Potts agreed that it was a near massacre. In his superbly laconic style he summed it up with the comment: "You could shoot with your eyes shut and kill a Cree." He left the battlefield with 19 scalps dangling from his belt. But these were not the trophies that were really valuable. The most important thing he won that day was imperishable fame as a warrior and war chief. His able and decisive leadership had carried the day, and the respect and honor he won would stand him in good stead again and again in the years to come.

With the barbarous work of scalping done and all the booty collected, the Piegans returned to their camp near Fort Kipp to celebrate their victory with a scalp dance. Potts, in his inscrutable way, returned to Fort Whoop-Up and resumed his work as a hunter and interpreter.

After passing a quiet winter at Whoop-Up, Potts was sent to Fort Spitzee in the spring of 1871. Following the departure of the wolfers from the country the post had been taken over by the traders. By this time Potts may have been wondering which of the two factions was the worse. He continued to see the misery the whisky traders were peddling to his people.

Firewater was destroying the Blackfoot as a people, turning once proud and fearless warriors into a race of whisky-sodden, skulking beggars. The country was unsafe for any man, red or white, and they all killed each other with mutual malice. Outside their forts the traders were prime targets of the Blackfoot. During the winter of 1871-1872, seven of them were killed by Piegans and Bloods while engaged in trading. In all instances the trading was for whisky. Indians were not safe anywhere. Victimized by the whiteman, they were killed by their own brothers. In that same winter Potts learned that some 70 Bloods were killed in drunken fights by their own relatives. Potts made frequent visits to the camp of his mother and witnessed some of the fights and killings firsthand.

CHAPTER FOUR

Wolf Pelts to Whisky Peddling

HARRY Taylor, like most men of his day, went west to seek adventure and fortune. But unlike most men he found them both, to a greater or lesser degree. Once he had arrived in the wild, wide-open country of the west he would never leave it. He tried his hand at everything from prospecting to proprietorship, and quickly learned that it was much easier to dig gold from the pockets of men than it was to dig it from the pockets of ore.

Taylor came to America in 1852 from England where he had been educated and trained for the spreading of the gospel. But once he had stepped ashore in the land of promise he found that his vocation was not a very lucrative one. Soon after he was enflamed with the stories of the riches to be made in the California goldfields. Making the long trip around the Horn to the west coast he spent six years at the diggings, but never did strike his bonanza.

In 1858 word of a new strike in the Cariboo country of British Columbia lured him to a fresher field where he hoped to find his golden pasture. Four years there told him that gold glittered no brighter in Canada than it did in the United States. Still determined, Taylor headed south again when he heard of the gold strikes in the Cascade Mountains of Idaho. For two years he picked and shoveled his way from Boise to Bannock, again with no luck.

After 12 years in the country things had just not panned out for him, so to speak. Despairing of ever finding the mother lode, he again headed for Canada where he had heard that there was money to be made in skins. He threw in with a bunch of Montanans who

(Above) "Kamouse" Taylor (second from left, standing, with white shirt) is pictured here with a group of his former rivals, the NWMP, at Fort Macleod in the 1880s. Taylor tried his hand at everything from preacher to whisky peddlar after his arrival in the Canadian northwest from England.

(Below) Run by the colorful and versatile Harry "Kamouse" Taylor, the Fort Macleod Hotel was a landmark of the Northwest in the 1880s.

assured him that there was money to be made in wolf skins. After a year or so with the ill-fated Spitzee Cavalry, he knew that he had been chasing the rainbow again. Those whisky traders in Prince Rupert's land were not to be fooled with. Whatever else he was, Harry was no fool. The whisky traders were making small fortunes, and if he could not beat them he would join them.

Along with Taylor's change in profession came a change in life. The time had come to settle down. He was soon smitten by a comely Blood maiden and approached her father for her hand. His offer of a trade musket, three Hudson's Bay Company blankets, two horses and a gallon of his horrid firewater did not impress the old man. But Harry was determined.

Sneaking into the Blood camp wearing a buffalo robe, Taylor stole the love of his life and made her his wife. For his feat he earned himself the Blood name "Kamouse"—thief—and the name stuck for the rest of his life. With his young bride Taylor travelled the country trading his whisky from the back of a wagon. His Blood wife was probably the only reason he survived his novice years as a trader.

In 1871 "Kamouse" and a negro named William Bond established a small whisky "fort" near High River. Their trading with Taylor's Blackfoot in-laws went well for a couple of years, but not so smoothly with other Indians of the area. In 1873 a band of Kootenais attacked their post and almost overran it. Help soon arrived from Whoop-Up and, in the celebration that followed, one of the Whoop-Up traders accidentally fired his gun into a keg of gunpowder and nearly finished the job the Kootenais had started.

With their fort in ruins, Taylor and Bond moved to Pine Coulee a few miles from Fort Whoop-Up. But their by now lucrative business was about to be ruined. The next year the North West Mounted Police arrived in the territory and the first reach of their long arm fell on the hapless head of "Kamouse." His buffalo robes were confiscated, his whisky poured onto the ground, and he was fined $200.

Poor Harry had to find another livelihood. He settled in the tiny town of Calgary that sprang up beside the NWMP post and started a modest restaurant. But again he was in the wrong place at the wrong time. Mounties ate in their fort, Indians ate in their teepees, and any others that came through the small river crossing were either too few or too poor to keep his restaurant in business.

Pulling up stakes again, he headed for Fort Macleod where he hoped business would be better. A growing, bustling town had sprang up around the headquarters of the NWMP and he built his Macleod Hotel on the town's main street. Before too long he also had a restaurant and a billiard hall going. After nearly 30 years Taylor had finally struck paydirt.

His Macleod Hotel was unique on the Canadian frontier and for many years a landmark in the town. What made it unique was not the impressive building, or its location in the wild frontier, but its proprietor. Whatever else could be said about Taylor it could never be said that he was colorless. He drew up a set of 30 rules and regulations for his customers which stated such things as: "Towels changed only once a week; every known fluid sold at the bar except water; baths furnished free down at the river; assaults on cook strictly forbidden; everything cash in advance; proprietor not accountable for anything; and all guests must rise by 6 A.M. as the bedsheets are needed for tablecloths."

Taylor's rules were the toast of the country and, encouraged by their reception, he drafted the "new ten commandments" for his restaurant and in doing so came as close as he would ever come to practising the ministry he was trained for. His restaurant was visited by some important people, one of them being Lord Latham, the Governor-General of Canada, who made a tour of the northwest in 1881. Looking over the menu in Kamouse's restaurant he saw soup listed. "What kind of soup?" the Lord asked. "Damn good soup!" Taylor replied.

In 1892 Taylor quit the restaurant-hotel business and retired to a small piece of land near Macleod where he grew a few crops and raised some cattle. He was never without friends who were always dropping by and he never disappointed them by letting them go away without hearing a yarn about his travels and adventures. He died on March 23, 1901. One of his friends eulogized him as a man "who may have been somewhat lacking in theoretical religion, but in the religion of humanity he was an able exponent . . ."

☆   ☆   ☆

While Potts was working for the whisky forts his mother had returned to live with her Blood relatives in the camp of her son, No Chief of the Many Fat Horses band. The band was under the leadership of an old and respected chief named Heavy Shield. In the same band was an Indian with the lengthy name of Not-Afraid-of-the-Gros Ventres, who was very wealthy owing to his having 10 wives and many daughters who brought him large payments for their marriages to successful young braves. Not-Afraid-of-the-Gros Ventres had formed his own group among the Many Fat Horses band and called it the Many Children band. This sub-band was fond of whisky and fighting and old Heavy Shield wanted nothing to do with them.

In the spring of 1872 the Many Fat Horses and the Many Children were camped together but, when the drinking sprees of the Many Children got to be excessively raucous, Heavy Shield moved his people a little further away. With him went Potts' mother and her son No Chief and his wife who was a daughter of Not-Afraid-of-the-Gros Ventres. The Many Children felt slighted at the move and were especially resentful of No Chief because they felt he was being shown favoritism.

When a member of the Many Children brought in a gallon of whisky for No Chief he sent word to the young man to come pick it up. When No Chief arrived he got into an argument with one of his brothers-in-law named Hairy Face. The Many Children had already been into the whisky and their resentment bubbled to the surface. As the quarrel became more heated and the taunting, belligerent warriors crowded around him, No Chief panicked and shot Hairy Face in the back. Enraged, Not-Afraid-of-the-Gros Ventres attacked his son-in-law. Defending himself, No Chief killed him with his knife. A third Indian, Big Snake, then jumped No Chief and the beleaguered brave stabbed him in the shoulder. As No Chief desperately tried to escape from the hostile ring of Indians another of his brothers-in-law shot and killed him.

Leaving No Chief's body on the ground for the dogs to eat, the Many Children went back to their drinking. A young boy went to Heavy Shield's camp and told Potts' mother what had happened. Getting her son's horse, Namo-pisi rigged up a travois and went over to the Many Children camp to get her son's body. Having packed up the body, she was about to ride away when she was pulled from her horse by the mis-named Good Young Man and brutally murdered.

It was several months before Potts learned of the killings. In the deliberate, calculating way of the Indian he brooded and planned his revenge. He was working as a wrangler at Fort Kipp at that time and he kept track of the whereabouts of the Many Children band and in particular the movements of Good Young Man. It was more than two months before he made his move to exact his revenge.

The Many Children had moved their camp into the valley of the Oldman River, not far from Fort Kipp. Potts kept an eye on the camp and a few days later while he was driving some horses down to the river he saw two Indians on a single horse headed for the fort. After watering the horses Potts was herding them back into the corral when the two Indians came out of the trading post and climbed aboard their horse. From the corral Potts recognized Good Young Man and another Blood named Morning Writing. Getting his

Winchester, he mounted up and followed them. Good Young Man saw him and spurred his overburdened horse on, hoping to reach the safety of his camp before the Metis caught up to him.

Potts gained on them and as he closed he steadied himself in the stirrups and fired twice from his galloping horse. Both shots missed, but as the Bloods reached the steep cutbank of the river their horse hesitated. Reining up, Potts jerked his rifle to his shoulder and snapped off a shot hitting Good Yound Man in the back and shattering his spine. Riding up to the riverbank he watched the Blood's body tumble down to the camp below. Morning Writing still sat on the horse, fretting as the half-blood eyed him. But Potts had no quarrel with the other man and allowed him to ride off.

Shortly after this incident Potts quit the whisky forts and returned to Montana. Disgusted by the havoc the traders and their firewater were having on his people, he never worked for them again. From this time on he would work against them. Although he was a notorious drinker himself, he never allowed the rotgut to control his life or drive him to brutal excesses such as that which had resulted in the deaths of his half-brother and mother.

Back in Montana, he returned to the camps of the Blackfoot, choosing the company of his wives' people, the Piegans, instead of the Bloods. He was probably wiser to stay clear of the Bloods for a while owing to the tensions his presence would have created.

Somehow the idle life of an Indian camp, in those days of reservations and restricted movement, was just not suited to a man like Potts. He was used to going where he wanted when he wanted, and doing exactly what he wanted along the way. Soon tiring of it, he again sought employment. In 1874 he went to work for the I.G. Baker trading company at their post on Badger Creek. While he knew that the Baker Company was responsible for running many of the whisky posts in Alberta, they were not in that business in Montana. The U.S. Army had put a stop to the illicit trade in guns and whisky and their trading business with the Montana Indians was for legitimate wares.

It might appear that Potts was settling into a quiet obscure life, but that was not the case. He was a born fighter and did not know the meaning of the word "quit." What he really wanted was to help destroy the leeching whisky traders although he had no direct means of doing it. It would not be too long however, before an assisting vehicle would come along.

During the early 1870s, while Potts was working for the whisky traders in Alberta, people in eastern Canada were clamoring for the takeover of the vast northwest territories by the Dominion. Before the sale of Prince Rupert's Land by the Hudson's Bay Company to the Government of Canada in 1869, Hudson's Bay agents had been spreading stories in the cities of the east about large gangs of American frontiersmen roaming the country at will and shooting it to pieces. At one point they claimed that more than 500 of these heavily-armed, lawless desperadoes roamed the northwest and, unless the Canadian government showed some legal presence in the territory, it was in dire danger of being annexed to the United States.

The stories may have been somewhat exaggerated, but the claims of the American presence and intentions in the northwest had a very real basis in fact. After Canada had asserted her claim to the territory and stopped the whisky trading, one Montana trader lamented: "If we had only been allowed to carry on the business in our own way for another two years, then there would have been none left to feed; whiskey, pistols and strychnine and other like processes would have effectively cleared away these natives."

But in the cities of eastern Canada government bureaucracy, haggling and indecision held up the appointment of any kind of official presence in the northwest for three years. And as politicians argued and procrastinated, rough and lawless men continued their unchecked ways on the plains of the west. An incident in 1873 was the catalyst that finally prodded the Canadian government from its collective inertia and led to the hasty formation of a police force that so many had called for.

CHAPTER FIVE

The Cypress Hills Massacre

ERHAPS one of the most important events in western Canadian
history was the fight between Indians and whites in 1873 that
has become known as the Cypress Hills Massacre. The term
massacre is a misnomer for the battle, however one-sided or
senseless, was fought between armed combatants. Its aftermath
created a great uproar in eastern cities, more than a little
international tension, and led to the formation of the North West
Mounted Police who brought law and order to the Canadian plains.

Events that led to the tragedy began in May 1873, when a party of
Canadian-American wolfers had their horses stolen from them on
the Teton River in northern Montana. After remounting, the wolfers
rode north across the border for the Cypress Hills where, they
believed, they would find the thieves. Their leader, John "Chief"
Evans of Spitzee Cavalry fame, rode at the head of a dozen
hardened, experienced plainsmen whose brushes with the Indians
in their wolf hunting ventures had done little to endear the redman
to them.

When Evans and his band arrived in the Cypress Hills they rode to
Battle Creek where two traders, Abel Farwell and Moses Soloman,
had trading posts and competed with each other for the trade of the
Indians. Nearby, a band of Assiniboines were camped under their
chief, Little Soldier. Evans went to Farwell's post and asked the
trader if the Indians had come in with any new horses lately.
Farwell told the wolfer that the Assiniboines had only five or six
horses in their whole camp. Disappointed at this news, the wolfers

Assiniboine Camp, Cypress Hills. It was a camp of Indians like this one that was the victim of the gang of American-Canadian wolfers in the Cypress Hills Massacre of 1873.

bedded down for the night.

The Assiniboines had observed the arrival of the wolfers and became a little unsettled over their presence. During the previous months the Indians of the area had been acting surly and had even threatened to kill Farwell and Soloman and destroy their posts. Only two days before the wolfers arrived an Indian from Little Soldier's camp had told a group of Metis that they intended to take everything the traders had and drive them out of the hills. If they resisted, the Assiniboine said, they would be killed.

The next day both the Indians and the wolfers began drinking early in the morning and grumbling about a fight. Tempers and whisky would prove to be a deadly combination. The spark that touched off the powderkeg came later that morning when one of the traders found that a horse that had been stolen from him a few days earler, and returned to him the previous morning, had been stolen again.

Grabbing his rifle, he asked the wolfers to accompany him to the Assiniboine camp and help him get his horse back. Determined to recover somebody's horse, the wolfers agreed to help him. When the Indians saw them coming they became resentful of the threatening manner in which they approached. They gathered around the whites and taunted them as Farwell questioned the drunken Little Soldier about the missing horse.

The chief assured Farwell that the horse was not in the camp. The Indians became angry and threatening. Women and children were sent scurrying into the brush behind the camp and the warriors began stripping as if preparing for battle.

The wolfers had thought they could intimidate the Indians, but when they could not their audacity turned to apprehension. They retreated from the camp and crowded into a coulee about 50 yards away. One of the wolfers, Thomas Hardwick, who had a reputation as a hardcase and was called the "Green River Renegade," shouted for Farwell to get out of the way so he could get a clear shot at the Indians. Farwell yelled for the Indians to scatter, then pleaded with the wolfers to go back to the fort.

The whites ignored his pleas and one of them fired into the still grouped Indians. Then all hell broke loose. Firing from the protection of the coulee the wolfers poured a withering fire into the exposed Assiniboines. Incensed and driven to recklessness by whisky, the Indians charged the wolfers' position three times before they retreated into the trees behind their camp to exchange fire from cover.

Evans and Hardwick rode to a small hill overlooking the Assiniboine position and began an effective flanking action.

Some of the Indians executed their own flanking action, and for a moment it looked as if the "Chief" and the "Green River Renegade" would be surrounded. Several of the wolfers, led by a Canadian named Ed Grace, rode to their aid. The first to the rescue, Grace was the first to die. He would be the only white casualty of the fight.

Seeing one of their own dead, the wolfers ceased fire and withdrew to Soloman's fort, which allowed them a commanding view of the Assiniboine camp, and they fired into it all afternoon. Unable to return to their lodges, the Indians scattered into the hills.

With the withdrawal of the Indians the wolfers went into the camp to pillage it. They found Chief Little Soldier, who was too drunk to flee, hiding in his teepee. A French Canadian named Vincent killed the helpless chief, cut off his head and stuck it on a pole as a trophy. A few women found left behind were raped by the whites, then killed along with some children that were found.

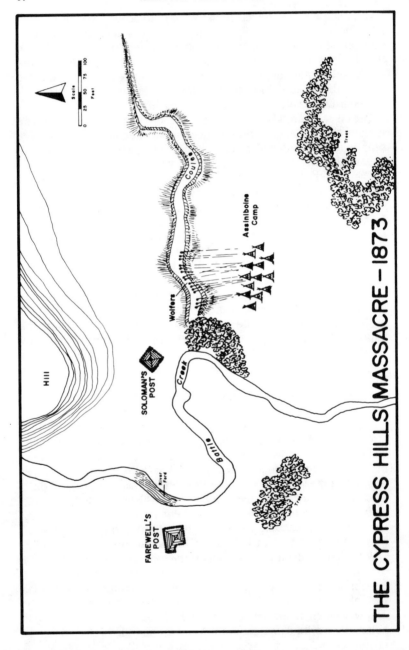

THE CYPRESS HILLS MASSACRE – 1873

In the morning the wolfers burned the Assiniboine camp around the slain bodies of the Indians. They buried their dead companion under the floor of Soloman's fort, then burned it to the ground to keep the Indians from mutilating the body. Such were the double standards of the frontiersman.

The wolfers never did find their stolen horses and eventually returned to Benton empty-handed. It was two years before any of the wolfers were brought to trial and when they were all were aquitted. The lives of almost 50 people were never vindicated, the only explanation of their deaths being hatred, whisky and a horse.

When news of the Cypress Hills Massacre, as it came to be called, reached the east it caused a great furor. Opinion that had been against establishing a law enforcement agency in the northwest waned, and Prime Minister John A. MacDonald hurriedly pushed through a bill which called for the formation of the North West Mounted Police. By October of 1873 parliament had enacted the bill that would see 300 red-coated, pill-box-hatted horsesoldiers sent west to quell the disturbances among the Indians and drive the gunslinging Americans out of Canada's newly acquired Northwest Territories.

It was not until the following year, however, that the force was ready to head out west. On June 6, 1874 the North West Mounted Police left Toronto for the wild plains of western Canada. Their orders were to make for the Whoop-Up country and eliminate the trade in whisky as well as any other trading that was not legal, establish and garrison forts in the region, and visit and impress upon the Indians of the area the power and good faith of the Government of Canada.

Heading up the newly-formed North West Mounted Police was Lt.-Col. George Atcheson French, Royal Canadian Artillery, who was appointed Commissioner. His second-in-command as Assistant Commissioner was another army man, Col. James Farquharson Macleod. Throughout the winter months of 1873-74, French and Macleod recruited and trained 300 men who would take the Queen's law to the western plains and impose it on the hundreds of whites and thousands of Indians in the territory. Late on the afternoon of July 8, 1874 the 300 red-coated, white-helmeted policemen-horsesoldiers formed up their mile and a half-long column of horses and riders, cannons and carts at Fort Dufferin on the Red River in Manitoba for the long march west.

From Toronto to Dufferin in Manitoba the travel had been easy for French and his police, most of it being done on American railroads. The 800 miles from Manitoba to Whoop-Up country were

Site of the Cypress Hills Massacre on Battle Creek. In the foreground (brush-covered area) stood Abel Farwell's fort. At center is Battle Creek and beyond is the clearing where the Assiniboines had their camp.

much more difficult. With Cree Metis guides the force set off west over trackless plains on a gruelling three-month-long march. Most of the men were easterners who were unaccustomed to wilderness travel, as were the horses and oxen that dragged the freight-laden Red River carts.

From the beginning, the Mounties had trouble. The logistics of such a march were staggering. After going only three miles it was realized that some of the supplies being hauled were extraneous while they were short of necessary ones. Some of the men also had second thoughts and several of them deserted after the first few miles.

The first days out the column followed the Boundary Commission trail along the 49th parallel and wood for campfires and water for stock and men was scarce. Poor rations prepared by inexperienced cooks did little to encourage men who suffered from heat which daily averaged about 90 degrees, and the ever present clouds of mosquitoes that were so thick they spotted the men's red tunics like raindrops. Most of the horses which were bred to the saddle were tiring quickly from the heat and the work of hauling carts and guns.

A week or so after their start the police were assaulted by a plague of grasshoppers and, for a day by hailstones "as large as walnuts." Forage for the horses was by now almost impossible to find. The men's rations grew worse and each day on the treeless, parched plains saw them caked with an "infernal" dust. One careless Mountie started a huge prairie fire, but luckily the wind was from the west and carried the flames away from them.

By the 19th of the month they had reached the Souris River in western Manitoba where they found fresh water, game and good forage for the horses for the first time since leaving Dufferin. After seven weeks on the trail, and having covered only 240 miles—less than 40 miles per week—French stopped at La Roche Percee to take stock of his column. The poorest animals and sickest men were sent north to Fort Ellice from whence they would continue on to Fort Edmonton along the well travelled Hudson's Bay Company trail. French and the rest of the column would continue west along the southern route.

After several days rest, French pushed on for the Bow and Belly rivers where he believed he would find the nefarious whisky traders. There, things got even worse. The country west was barren and dry, there was little grass, his Metis guides did not know the country, and his maps were highly inaccurate. The march would become a gruelling trek through dusty, hot, waterless wilderness.

Almost another month passed before the force reached its destination. There they were greeted with disappointment when they found that the whisky forts were not where they were supposed to be. By now most of the men were severely weakened and the horses and oxen were all but done in. French intended to head north for Edmonton, but his guides advised him that he would never make it. His only chance they said, would be to head south to the Sweetgrass Hills on the U.S. border where they would find good grazing and water. It took them two weeks of staggering travel to reach the hills, leaving a trail of dead horses and oxen behind them.

In the Sweetgrass Hills they found water, wood, grass and shelter, and both stock and men recuperated quickly. But their Metis guides refused to go any farther into Blackfoot country and the Mounties found themselves stranded. (If the truth be fully stated the Redcoats were lost.)

On September 22, Commissioner French, Assistant Commissioner Macleod and a small party headed south for Benton where they intended to "communicate with the Government, receive instructions and obtain some necessary supplies of oats, moccasins, socks etc."

When the eastern Canadians rode into the raw frontier town of Benton, they were awed by the log cabin metropolis of the American northwest that was derisively known as the "sagebrush Sodom." The town was a huddled collection of rough-hewn, unpainted log shacks and buildings; most of them saloons and gambling houses that never shut their doors. The streets were

I.G. Baker Company, Benton, Montana. Potts was working for this firm when he was offered to the Mounties as a scout when the NWMP straggled into the Montana town tired and lost in the fall of 1874.

infested with the rough breed of the frontier: wolfers, blacklegs, outlaws, Indians, traders, and general, all-around hardcases. As they made their way through the slick, mud-rutted streets, they noticed the white sprinkles of the playing cards of the previous night's gambling.

As supplies were their main concern, the policemen naturally sought the premises of the I.G. Baker Company, the largest mercantile firm in town. At the counter of the general store they found Charles Conrad, a former Confederate Cavalry officer who at once had some empathy for the bedraggled horsemen from the north. Upon learning who they were and why they had come west, Conrad seemed delighted. He said it was a great satisfaction to know that the law had finally come to the Canadian west, and he went out of his way to accommodate the Canadians. In truth, Conrad probably was not pleased so much by the fact that the NWMP had come to curtail the traffic in whisky as he was by the knowledge that they would eliminate the competition to his company from the small, independent traders.

Conrad supplied the policemen with all their needs, and when Commissioner French explained, as delicately as he could, their situation in the Sweetgrass Hills, the trader offered them what was probably the best thing that happened to them since their arrival in the country—a guide. He told them that they would need a man who knew both the country and the Indians well. And he had just the man for them: a man who knew the country as well as he knew his own face, was half Blackfoot, and was well known and respected among the Indians.

French and his men thought this was the best piece of luck they had stumbled upon since heading west. But when Jerry Potts walked into the store they were not so sure. They were not very impressed with the short, bow-legged, slope-shouldered little man who stepped through the door. He looked almost comical as he stood there holding a Winchester '73 rifle that was nearly as long as he was, and the incongruous little bowler hat he wore just did not belong with the greasy buckskins and moccasins. The fact that Potts did not offer much conversation did not do much to inspire confidence either. Yet the Canadians were in no position to be critical. They graciously, albeit reluctantly, accepted the services of the diminuitive guide.

French questioned Conrad about the location of Fort Whoop-Up and was surprised to learn that it was not where he had thought it was. They had been laboring under the mistaken assumption that the whisky fort was at the junction of the Bow and Belly rivers, but Conrad pointed out that it was at the forks of the St. Mary's and Belly rivers. They would need a guide indeed.

Asking about the numerous so-called whisky "forts," he was again surprised to learn that with the exception of one or two they were not really forts at all. Any trader's log cabin or soddy from which he plied his wares to the Indians was considered a "fort." French realized the he had a lot to learn about the west, but he was not sure that the man he had accepted as his guide could teach it to him.

Loading their provisions, the NWMP departed Fort Benton and returned to the Sweetgrass Hills. There, French took half the force and continued northeast into Saskatchewan country where he would establish the force headquarters at Swan River. Colonel Macleod took command of the remainder of the force with orders to proceed to Fort Whoop-Up, expel the whisky traders, and establish a western outpost.

Macleod was no more confident of his guide's competance than French had been. He questioned Potts about the location and state of Fort Whoop-Up and what kind of resistance they could expect. Potts told him that there were no whisky traders left there. They had all pulled out when they heard that the police force was headed west. Macleod had reluctantly accepted everything else the Metis had told him, but this was too much. Of course there were whisky traders at Fort Whoop-Up. Their gruelling three-month march over the trackless wilderness was all aimed at their busting the bastion of

American contempt and lawlessness on Canadian soil.

Still skeptical of his tongue-tied little guide, Macleod set out from the Sweetgrass HIlls, headed northwest. Any reservations they had about Potts were quickly dispelled however. Sam Steele, who was a Sub-Inspector with the force when they rode out of the Sweetgrass Hills on the morning of October 4, 1874, later wrote: "He won the confidence of all ranks the first day out." Riding out far ahead of the column Potts was often out of their sight though they were never out of his.

At noon, when they reached Milk River, they found their guide on the riverbank, hunkered down over the dressed carcass of a buffalo cow. Potts grunted at them to join him for dinner. The next day the scout turned the column sharply to the northwest, following along Milk River Ridge, and led it to an excellent campsite with plenty of grass, firewood and some of the best springwater in the country—certainly the best the policeman had tasted since leaving civilization. As Steele put it: "To those new to such life he appeared to know everything."

Later that day they met a couple of wagons being driven by Americans who were headed back from the Whoop-Up country. Macleod searched the wagons but found only buffalo robes. He felt certain that the robes had been bought with whisky and was more sure than ever that the country was crawling with whisky peddlers. Potts, on the other hand, was even more convinced that there were none left.

During the night of their second day out the policemen slept fitfully as a mysterious rumbling could be heard all through the night. When they awoke they found themselves surrounded by a great herd of buffalo. Men grabbed their rifles as they rolled out of their blankets, but Potts was moving among the greenhorns, warning them not to fire or unduly disturb the huge, shaggy beasts. If they did, he cautioned, the buffalo would stampede and horses, oxen, Red River carts and policemen would become prairie fertilizer.

Hundreds of the animals had crowded down into the coulee where the men were camped and thousands more cluttered the plains around. The great creatures had to be carefully hazed back from the springs so that the policemen and their stock could drink. Quietly breaking camp the troopers formed up their column and Potts led them in a waving caravan through the dense, rolling sea of brown hides. All day long they rode through it, the easterners amazed by its immense size. Every now and then a young bull would snort and feint at a horse or oxen, but Potts' warning was

It was a relieved and weary column of lost Redcoats that Jerry Potts led out of the Sweetgrass Hills of Montana into the Whoop-Up country in October 1874.

heeded and later that day he led the column out of the herd onto the open prairie.

Towards evening they came across the bullet-riddled body of a scalped Assiniboine, lying beside the trail. Macleod asked Potts what he thought had happened. In his classic laconic style Potts explained with one word: "Drunk." Macleod knew he had to be satisfied with this brief explanation.

A few days later the NWMP reached Fort Whoop-Up. The palisaded post with its loop-holed blockhouses was an impressive sight to Macleod's military eye. But he was not as impressed with the homespun Stars and Stripes that fluttered above it. The fort was also strangely quiet. He still believed that it was full of gun-toting whisky traders and that they were waiting in ambush for him. With crisp military precision, Macleod had the two nine-pounder cannons and pair of mortars swung into position on the west side of the fort atop the hill they had halted on. Orders were barked and the Redcoats formed into battle positions. Potts slouched in his saddle, calmly watching all the preparation.

When the silence persisted Macleod rode up to his guide and asked him to approach the quiet fort with him. Reaching the gates the policeman pounded on the heavy wood and waited for them to open. Slowly the thick doors swung back and a goateed old man poked his shaggy head out. Instead of being met with resistance, Macleod was extended an invitation. Inside the fort Macleod found few people, just as Potts said he would. Their host was Dave Akers, who was running the post in the absence of his boss, D.W. Davis. Besides the proprietor there were only a couple of Blackfoot squaws on the premises. Akers politely invited Macleod and his officers in for lunch and served them a tasty meal of buffalo steaks and fresh vegetables from the fort's garden.

Macleod's frustration at this turn of events is understandable. After three months of foot-slogging travel he was hoping to find something worthwhile at the end of the line. If he learned anything from his first adventure in the west it was that his unimposing looking scout was to be trusted and believed. He was convinced that Potts was worthy of the trust and confidence expressed in him by Conrad. He offered the Metis a job as interpreter and guide at a rate of pay of $90 a month. Potts accepted.

Macleod was practical about being left alone in a country he knew nothing about, even if he had lacked complete confidence in his guide. He knew he needed the skills and knowledge of a man like Potts, even if he did suspect they were somewhat limited. Potts saw the offer as a means to strike back at the whisky traders and rid the Blackfoot people of them.

The policemen then faced the chore of finding a suitable site for the construction of a fort from which to operate. This time when Macleod asked Potts' advice he accepted it with less reservation. Potts said he knew just the place.

He led the straggling column of tired men, winded horses and oxen, and squeaking carts to an island in the Old Man River, about 30 miles northwest of Fort Whoop-Up. The island was about 600 acres in size, large enough to hold the fort and graze the horses and cattle the policemen had with them. There was plenty of pasture, groves of cottonwoods for building purposes, and plenty of game roamed the plains nearby. The island was also strategically located near an important river crossing of the Blackfoot.

Warned by dipping temperatures, Macleod immediately put his men to work building a stable for their nearly exhausted horses. Some of them were in such bad shape that he did not believe they would make it through the winter unless they had plenty of good grass in a well sheltered pasture. Potts suggested that such a place

(Above) Fort Whoop-Up. Seen from the interior, this is how the famous whisky fort looked just before the arrival of the NWMP in the area.
(Below) This Blackfoot village was situated near an island in the Old Man River not far from Fort Macleod.

could be found in Montana, at Sun River.

It was a journey of 200 miles, again through unknown country. Macleod asked Potts to guide Insp. James M. Walsh and a detachment of men with 64 of the worst horses, 20 oxen and 10 head of cattle to the Sun River country to spend the winter. Potts would also use the trip to go back to Benton and get his wives and family and bring them back.

Just as he was preparing to leave on October 29, a Blackfoot chief named Three Bulls came to the police camp and complained that a negro named William Bond had a whisky post at a place called Pine Coulee, about 50 miles north. The Indian said that Bond had sold him two gallons of bad rotgut for two of his best horses. He also said that the negro had a large whisky cache in the area.

CHAPTER SIX

Crowfoot

MACLEOD could hardly contain his excitement. Here at last was a chance to get about the work he had come west to do. He knew he had to be careful if he wanted his first action against the lawless whisky traders to be successful. The police camp had become an overnight attraction in the isolated country, and wandering whites and Indians were drifting through it all day long. Any of them, Macleod knew, could be in the whisky business, and any loose-tongued remarks made by him could mean the loss of his expected capture. Summoning Potts, he explained Three Bulls' complaint and told the scout to be ready to ride out with the Indian at daybreak.

He then instructed Insp. Lief N. Crozier to pick 10 of his best men and meet Potts on the trail. When the policemen moved out late that night they did not know what their assignment was to be. Macleod was determined that his first strike at the lawbreakers would be a complete success.

After meeting Potts and Three Bulls, Crozier's detachment rode northwest. Two days later they were back with four whitemen and Bond in tow. The five traders had two wagons loaded with whisky in their possession, as well as 116 buffalo robes, 16 horses, five Henry repeating rifles and five Colt revolvers. The whisky was promptly poured on the ground by a very satisfied Assistant Commissioner. The buffalo robes, horses and guns were confiscated.

In his capacity as justice of the peace, Macleod convened court on the spot and found the culprits guilty of trafficking in contraband. Three of the men who were merely hired hands were fined $50 each, while Bond and the other man, who turned out to be none other than Harry "Kamouse" Taylor, of Spitzee Cavalry fame, were fined $200 each.

The next day, as Potts was preparing to leave with Inspector Walsh and the horse herd for Sun River, a Mr. Weatherwax, better known to his friends as "Waxey", arrived from Benton. Upon hearing that some of his "friends" were in custody he paid their fines—all exept Bond's. Macleod suspected that he did not pay the negro's fine because he was the only one actually implicated in the whisky trading by Three Bulls. Potts knew Weatherwax and Taylor well from earlier years and warned Macleod that he would probably have more trouble from them in the future. The policeman salted away the information but had to release Taylor and the others. Bond was confined to a makeshift stockade that the police had hastily thrown up.

Potts left with Inspector Walsh and the horses the following day. After guiding them to their wintering grounds at Sun River, he went on to Benton where he gathered his family and his own horse herd and returned to the Oldman River. Upon arriving he went to see Macleod and told him of some facts and rumors he had heard on his trip.

The Blackfoot had been conspicuously absent from the area of the police camp since the arrival of the NWMP, and Potts explained that it was due to stories having been spread among the Indians by the whisky traders just before their hasty flight. They had told the Indians that the Mounties, as the policemen were now being called, had come into the country to do the same thing to the Blackfoot that the "Longknives" were doing to the Sioux across the border. Potts also said that the traders believed the Mounties would only be in the country for the winter. Many of them had cached their stores of whisky in the Whoop-Up country intending to return to them once the policemen had left.

As much as he would have liked to dismiss the rumors, Macleod had lately come to believe the Metis scout when he told him something. He asked Potts to go among the Blackfoot camp and try to dispell their impressions of why the police were in the country. He was also to try to learn if there was any real substance to the stories of the whisky traders' caches. During the last weeks of November, 1874, Potts travelled to the scattered camps of the Bloods, Piegans and Blackfoot, explaining the presence of the NWMP and gaining assurances from the Indians that they would

(Left) Col. James F. Macleod. Assistant Commissioner of the NWMP. Macleod built the first police post in the Northwest and both it and the town which sprang up around it were named after him.

(Right) Crowfoot, head chief of the Siksika of the powerful Blackfoot Confederacy during the restless and troublesome times of the settling of the Canadian Northwest.

(Below) Sun River, Montana Territory. It was to this relative plenty of pasture and shelter that Potts took the near emaciated horses of the NWMP for the winter of 1875-75 after their gruelling trek across the Canadian plains.

deal with the police in peace. When he returned to the police camp he reported to Macleod that he had visited all the major bands and that it was up to the Indians to come to them.

During his absence, Fort Macleod, as the Mounted Police post had been named, had been nearly completed. Most of the Mounties were under barracks roofs, the remaining stock were in stables, and the force was well-provisioned for the coming winter. Conrad's supply wagons had recently arrived from Benton after pressing through a raging blizzard in which they had lost 30 oxen.

The month of November was almost gone before any of the Blackfoot confederacy entered into the newly constructed Fort Macleod. A couple of days before December a small group of Bloods and Piegans hesitantly rode into the post to see what the strange Redcoats were all about. Macleod was delighted that some of the Indians had finally showed up. He received them with all the pomp and officiousness of his office, then herded them into his quarters where he hoped to be convinced of their sincerity.

Potts was summoned to interpret the proceedings. The Indians, in their characteristic style, expounded at length. Macleod in his eagerness found their longwindedness almost trying, but he sat in patience and endured their almost endless tirade. Finally the Indians were finished and, with relief and expectation, Macleod turned to Potts and asked him what they had said. Potts, with typical brevity, summed up the whole of the Indians' speech with one phrase: "Dey damn glad you're here."

A couple of days later a young Blackfoot brave rode into the post and told Macleod that Chief Crowfoot wanted to visit the white chief. All the Blackfoot chief wanted was an assurance from the chief of the Redcoats that he could come in peace. From Potts, Macleod learned that Crowfoot or "Isapo-muxika," head chief of the Siksika of the Blackfoot confederacy, was probably the most important and influential of all the Blackfoot chiefs. If Macleod could win his support the work of the police would be made much easier. His leadership and diplomacy prevented on the Canadian plains a scene that was painfully recurrent on the prairies south of the border between whites and Indians. But he was not simply a blanket Indian. He was also a warrior who had won the respect and admiration of his people by his courage and fierceness in battle. Where he differed from other chiefs was in his wisdom. He knew that his people had to co-operate with the whites or perish.

Crowfoot was not born a Siksika but was the son of a Blood warrior. Two years after his birth in 1830, his father was killed in a raid on the Crows and, in 1835, his mother married a Blackfoot

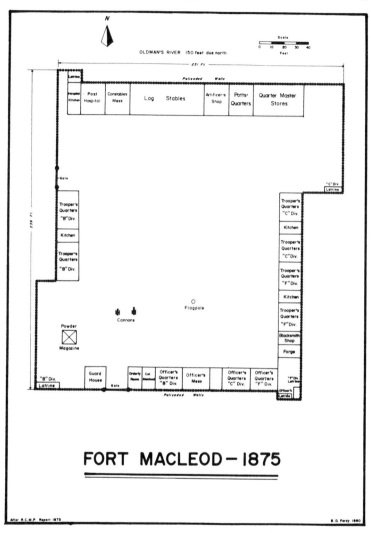

FORT MACLEOD — 1875

warrior who took them to live in the land of the Siksika. There he was given the name Bear Ghost, "Kyiah-sta-oh," by his step-father.

When he was old enough to accompany the warriors on raids he accounted for himself well and earned the name "Isapo-mixika" —Crow Indian's Big Foot—which the whites soon shortened to Crowfoot. As a young warrior he went on many raids and was involved in some 20 fights in which he received six wounds. Before long his reputation as a warrior saw him leading his own raiding and war parties, which made him respected among the tribe. By 1850 he was being recognized as a war chief.

With each year the Blackfoot became more and more aware that their country was being surrounded by the whites. To the north and east the Hudson's Bay Company enticed them to trade, while from the south came the American Fur Company. However, they were still fairly isolated from the whites, having the Crees and Assiniboines to the north and east, and the Bloods and Piegans to the south, as buffers against white expansionism. But, by 1865, things had changed. The whites no longer remained in their forts waiting for the Indians to come to them. Rather, they ventured into Blackfoot country, bringing their whisky and guns. Some of the things they brought the Blackfoot needed, others they would have been better off without.

Just as the whites began their invasion of Blackfoot territory their old and powerful chief Three Suns died, and the tribes looked about for a new leader. Crowfoot was seen as a prime candidate, but the chieftainship of a tribe usually fell to a family lineage. Three Suns' son was not accepted by all as being strong enough to lead the tribe, and eventually the Siksika split itself down the middle in its allegiances.

Late in 1865 the Blackfoot were attacked on Battle River by the Crees. A savage, two-day-long fight ensued. Camped several miles away was Crowfoot who, upon hearing of the battle, rallied his forces and went to the aid of the besieged camp. His able leadership turned the tide of battle and the Crees, who still greatly outnumbered the Blackfoot, were badly beaten. This incident convinced many of those who had been opposing Crowfoot to support him, and soon after he became undisputed leader of the Blackfoot tribe.

With the close of the 1860s, Crowfoot saw a big change in his land and his people. White traders were all over the country, destroying the Indians with firewater and guns. The poisonous whisky turned father against son, brother against brother, and each winter saw dozens of Indians kill each other in drunken orgies.

On December 1, 1874, Crowfoot and his Blackfoot entered Fort Macleod. Coached by Potts, Macleod received Crowfoot with all the decorum demanded by his position. Again there was a lengthy and somewhat impassioned speech which Macleod dutifully endured. During the chief's oratory Macleod recognized a few Blackfoot words he had learned and was pleased to hear Crowfoot mention

(Above) Fort Macleod was the first Mountie post built in the Northwest—on an island in the Old Man River.
(Below) The town of Fort Macleod was built nearby on the banks of the river.

"napi-okee," which meant whisky, and "napi-kwan" which meant white man. From the distinguished chief's gestures and expressions Macleod assumed that he was expressing his praise and gratitude to the NWMP. When the chief finished his speech Macleod turned to Potts with a sense of satisfaction and anticipation.

Jerry Potts; scout, guide, interpreter and general hell-raiser with the NWMP.

Potts' translation of Crowfoot's monologue took only moments, and did nothing to sate Macleod's bated breath. The Assistant Commissioner was no doubt a little piqued by his interpreter's lack of loquaciousness, but he was learning more and more to accept the fact that Potts' red blood had gone to his white tongue.

A few days later Macleod was placated when Crowfoot, Red Crow of the Bloods, and Bull's Head of the Piegans all came into the fort to hold a grand council. Potts, who had been instrumental in setting up the pow-wow, carefully instructed Macleod in the proper procedure for receiving the chiefs. Nothing, he said, could be discussed before all ceremony was observed, including shaking hands, sharing prayers and smoking the pipe.

Macleod had come to completely trust in his unassuming interpreter and guide. When the three chiefs, accompanied by hundreds of well-armed and regal looking braves, arrived, Macleod was the perfect host, He followed Potts' directions to the letter and the chiefs were favorably impressed. After the preliminaries were properly dispensed with, the four chiefs got down to business.

Crowfoot rose and eagerly shook hands with Macleod and his officers. The other chiefs followed his lead, then the Blackfoot chief began to speak and even those who could not understand the language knew that his words were sincere. He thanked the great spirit and the great grandmother for sending the Redcoats to save them from the ravages of the cursed firewater and the cheating traders. He expressed his faith in the police and promised to live with them in peace. When he finished Red Crow and Bull's Head endorsed his words, thanking the police for their presence and telling how they had been robbed and ruined by the whisky traders; how their wives and daughters had been turned into prostitutes; how their horses had been stolen and they could no longer follow the buffalo; how their young men were killing each other in drunken fights.

When it was Macleod's turn to speak he told the chiefs that the great grandmother had sent the police into the land of the Blackfoot to enforce the law. There would be only one law and Indians and whites alike would be punished for breaking it. He impressed on them again that they had not come to take the Blackfoot's land, and whenever the great chiefs of the whites wished to do something in the land of the Blackfoot, word would be sent to the chiefs before it was done.

As the speeches were finished Potts translated them. His translation of Blackfoot into English was brief and concise, but one Mountie said: "The chief difficulty about his interpretations was that, after he had interpreted from the Blackfoot into the English language, you weren't very much farther ahead, for his English was weird." When he worked from English to Blackfoot he showed all the verbosity and passion of his Indian blood. As one observer put it: "When he translated from English to Blackfoot his eyes gleamed as if his soul were in it, and as if showing that he felt that every word of it was good for the Indians." This paradox of Potts' oratory prowess made him the perfect diplomat when dealing with the Blackfoot. He knew that the Indians indulged in long speeches out of respect; the whites did it out of vanity.

The council was a huge success. Both Crowfoot and Macleod were sincere in what they said and the meeting proved to be a momentous one. In all the years of hardship and unrest that were to follow, the Blackfoot would never cause the Mounties any large scale trouble. Any that did occur was the result of the actions of renegades or individuals, white and red, and neither Macleod or Crowfoot could ever fault each other for going back on their words given at the first council to be held between the Blackfoot chiefs and Canadian authorities.

As one chief said: "Before you came the Indian crept along, now he is not afraid to walk erect." Bull's Head was so impressed with Macleod that he gave the Mountie his own name, "Stamix-oto-kan," and he was always proud that he had done so, never having to be ashamed of the white man upon whom he had bestowed his name.

The Blackfoot chiefs left the council pleased and Potts was elevated a few steps in Macleod's estimation. He had seen another side of the Metis' inestimable character and the contrasts of the man must have been impressive while at the same time vexatious.

The day after the council, as Macleod was congratulating himself for his greatest triumph since arriving in Blackfoot territory, he experienced his greatest setback. His only prisoner since his arrival, the negro Bond, escaped that evening as he was being taken to the latrine. A guard wounded the negro as he made his break, but he succeeded in getting away. Macleod was furious. He had detailed three men to be with the prisoner at all times, but on this occasion there was only one. He unceremoniously busted the three men to the ranks.

Smarting from the loss of his prisoner, the Colonel was appeased a few days later when he acquired a second. After all the words and promises of the council with the Blackfoot chiefs, he found himself with the opportunity to prove the worth of both his own platitudes and those of the Indians.

Shortly after the December conference at Fort Macleod, the

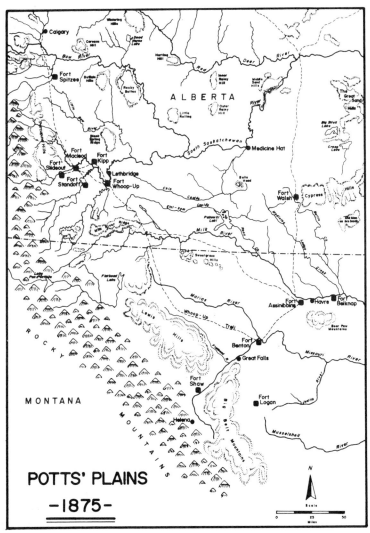

POTTS' PLAINS
—1875—

Blackfoot sent word that they wanted to hold a feast in honor of the Mounties' arrival in Blackfoot territory. Potts explained that the invitation could not be refused, and refreshed Macleod and his officers as to how they should behave in the presence of the chiefs. When the Colonel and a party of his officers rode out to the Blackfoot camp they were received with the Indians' finest hospitality. After the customary greetings, words of praise and smoking of pipes the festivities began.

As the feasting and dancing progressed the Indians became increasingly avid with their performance. Whisky, of course, could not be tolerated when the police were around so the Indians drank strong tea laced with black tobacco. Although it did not have the kick of firewater it had some effect as a stimulant. The dancing became more and more riotous and an old Indian grew jealous, watching his comely young squaw dancing with a young brave. The old man left the teepee where the dancing was taking place and returned minutes later with his rifle. Cutting a slit in the teepee from the outside he poked his rifle through and shot his young wife dead. The woman fell across the fire right in front of where the Mounties were sitting.

The killing created a dangerous situation as relatives of both families quickly gathered around the lodge. Lining up in opposing ranks they began to challenge one another. Macleod was faced with his first chance to show the Indians that what he had told them at the conference was the truth. Summoning all his powers of diplomacy he convinced the Indians to hand the killer over to him and promised that he would be punished. The old man was sent to Winnipeg for trial and sentenced to a prison term at Stoney Mountain penitentiary. The Blackfoot were satisfied that they could trust the Redcoats to keep their word.

In the coming years as the buffalo disappeared and the Blackfoot were confined to reservations and became dependent on the whites, this pledge of honor was sorely tested. Forced to protect and to provide for his people, Crowfoot's loyalty was tried on several occasions when the NWMP came for lawbreakers who sought refuge in his camps. But always his good sense got the better of his outraged instincts and he never lifted a hand in violence to the Redcoats.

The greatest test came with the Riel Rebellion, in 1885, when conditions on the reserve were the worst they had ever been and Crowfoot was constantly besieged with entreaties to join the Cree and Metis in their war with the whites. The rebels made promises of plunder and a return to the old ways of the free life and the buffalo hunt. The prospects were inviting for the impoverished Blackfoot, but when the government moved to alleviate some of their hardship and promised more help to come, Crowfoot decided to remain loyal to the Crown.

With the end of the Northwest Rebellion, Prime Minister John A. MacDonald made a trip out west to pay a visit to the Blackfoot chief who had remained loyal to his government. He met the chief at Blackfoot Crossing in 1886 and Crowfoot told him he would like to repay his visit by going east. In September he and several other Blackfoot chiefs travelled east on the iron horse and made a two-week tour of cities like Ottawa, Montreal and Quebec City. What he saw there only confirmed what he had always believed: The whites were too numerous and powerful to resist. The only way his people would survive was to accept their ways and live in harmony with them.

After his return west the chief's health began to fail and he spent most of the winter sick in his lodge. By 1888 he was on his back more than he was on his feet. In the summer of that year he travelled to Montana where, for one last time, he acted as peacemaker between the Bloods and Piegans and their old enemies, the Assinboines and Gros Ventres. Early in 1890 his health had deteriorated so much that he was completely bedridden. On April 22 he slipped into a coma and three days later the great Blackfoot warrior, chief, statesman and peacemaker died.

CHAPTER SEVEN

The Winter Of 1875

L ATE in December 1874, Potts was sent to guide Superintendent Brisbois and 13 Mounties to Fort Kipp, about 50 miles southeast of Fort Macleod, where they were to spend the winter. Macleod's excuse was that there was not enough hay for all the horses, but what he really wanted was to be rid of Brisbois. A French Canadian, Brisbois had a falling out with the Assistant Commissioner while Fort Macleod was being built and Macleod accused him of insubordination. The two were to be rivals the rest of their careers. Macleod did not like the independent Brisbois, some suggested, because he was French. A year later, when Brisbois was sent to establish a fort on the Red Deer River at Blackfoot Crossing, Macleod changed its name—which had been christened after Brisbois, to one he liked better—Calgary.

With Brisbois and his detachment settled in, Potts returned to Fort Macleod to continue his work of soothing the Blackfoot and encouraging their trust in the NWMP. As he rode from camp to camp, Potts observed the beginning of another great change in his beloved plains. A few years earlier he had seen the whisky traders invade Blackfoot country and lay it and the Indians waste with whisky. As the winter wore on he saw a new, albeit peaceable, threat creep into the land of the Blackfoot: The plains were becoming settled.

As Christmas passed and the new year slowly began, he watched a small village spring up around the NWMP fort. Two or three stores were rapidly erected, the largest belonging to the I.G. Baker

Company. A billiard hall was hastily nailed together and it became a favorite haunt of the policemen during their off-duty hours. A barber shop and a shoe store were also opened, both being run by ex-Mounties. Booze, although unlawful, was not unknown in the backwoods berg and some of the most fervent users of the "bottled devil" were the NWMP themselves. Even Macleod was not unknown to spend some of his free time enjoying a toddy or two. Stories of his two-fisted drinking bouts are a matter of record and a regular companion on these excursions of diversion was his gruff little scout, Jerry Potts.

The late months of winter 1875 were bitterly cold and excruciatingly boring for the NWMP at Fort Macleod. Heavy winter clothing had not arrived so Macleod ordered that the buffalo robes confiscated from Taylor and Bond be made into coats. About their boredom, the Colonel could do very little. The men tried to keep themselves occupied and warm by playing winter sports, even a snowy version of cricket, but their complaints continued, frequently and loud. Their pay had not arrived, the food was lousy, and the whole outlook generally bleak. It got so bad for some that 18 decided to desert en masse and head for the goldfields of Montana where stories of the riches to be made were like the promise of salvation.

It was during this first long winter that Potts showed the NWMP another of his seemingly unlimited skills, one which completely amazed them by its uncanniness, and contributed to making him a legend as the best scout and guide in the Canadian-American northwest. The absolute confidence expressed in him by the whites and Indians who knew him had not yet been completely accepted by the NWMP. Granted, he had led them to Whoop-Up country, finding excellent campsites along the way, had chosen a perfect spot for the establishment of their western headquarters, and knew the ways and had the respect of the Indians of the country; but the policemen placed little faith in the stories about his skills that many claimed were almost supernatural.

Early in February, 1875, Potts was assigned to guide Inspector Crozier and 10 men to the Bow River where they were to arrest some American whisky traders who had a cache in the area. The Mounties included Sgt. W.D. Antrobus, who left an account of the journey and described Potts' uncanny ability to go from one point to another, even in a blinding blizzard. From the time the party left Fort Macleod they experienced bad weather. The temperature was so cold that Antrobus commented: "Even Jerry Potts, although he remained rolled up in his blankets, did not sleep at all."

Potts led the NWMP through storm after storm and never once hesitated because he was unsure of the way. The trail took them to a cabin on Lee Creek. Quietly moving in on it, the policemen kicked open the door to find three whitemen hunched over a small table playing cards and drinking whisky. Two Blackfoot squaws were also in the cabin. After searching the place the NWMP found a large store of whisky which Crozier spilled into the snow. The three men, one of whom was "Waxey" Weatherwax, whom Potts had warned Macleod about a few months earlier, were placed under arrest and taken back to Fort Macleod.

On their return journey the party ran into a savage snowstorm in which visibility was at times no more than 100 feet. "We could not be guided by the wind," Antrobus reported, "because it did not blow five minutes at a time from the same direction." As the storm worsened the party became separated, with Potts in one group and Antrobus in the other. Within minutes Antrobus was lost and decided to sit and wait out the storm. In a matter of moments his tracks were obliterated. He could not see more than 30 yards away. The sergeant had almost resigned himself and his men to certain death when, through the swirling snow, they saw Potts, trudging through the drifts towards them. With Potts leading, they rejoined the other group which the scout had told to stay put. Wasting no time, Potts set out across the snow-screened plains southward, where he struck the Highwood River at a point not a mile above the spot where they had camped on their way north to Lee Creek.

How Potts could have accomplished such a feat the NWMP were at a loss to explain. Yet, in his years with the force, he repeated such feats over and over again. Sam Steele, with whom Potts worked closely for many years, perhaps explained it as well as any one could: "He possessed an uncanny sense of locality and direction. Others could guide travellers through country they had visited before, but this man could take a party from place to place by the quickest route, through country altogether unknown to him, without compass and without sight of the stars. Unlike other guides, he never talked with others when he was at work. He would ride on ahead by himself, keeping his mind fixed on the mysterious business of finding the way. He was never able to give any clear explanation of his method. Some mysterious power, perhaps a heritage from his Indian ancestors, was at work."

When Crozier and Antrobus reached Fort Macleod they related the story of Potts' remarkable trail sense to the Assistant Commissioner. Macleod listened intently but passed off much of their enthusiasm about the scout's skill as being an overreaction to their recent ordeal. He did not know that he was about to experience firsthand the unusual homing instincts of his Metis guide.

In March, Macleod received word that he was to travel to Helena, Montana and meet Inspector Irvine who was coming out to the American territorial capital to begin extradition proceedings against the wolfers who had been involved in the Cypress Hills Massacre of 1873. Helena was about 120 miles southwest of Benton, again in country the NWMP knew nothing about. Macleod summoned Potts.

The Colonel picked three men to accompany him, besides the ubiquitous Potts. Insp. Cecil Denny, Sergeant Cochrane and Sub-Const. Charles Ryan would go with him. The five men left Fort Macleod on March 15, leading packhorses loaded with blankets, tea, bacon and hardtack—but no tent. Macleod and his men were in high spirits as they left the post on their 300-mile-long journey. They had good reason to be light-hearted. They had arrived in Whoop-Up country, stopped the trade in whisky, won the confidence of the Indians, and weathered a miserable winter. As they rode down the St. Mary's River, all could feel the approach of spring and thoughts of the long, hard winter were left behind. They had no idea that the most trying ordeal of the winter was yet to come.

Their first night out, they reached Fort Whoop-Up and again were treated to the hospitality of old Dave Akers. As they were leaving the next morning, the wizened trader pointed to the sun and two rainbow-like halos that ringed it. He called the halos sun dogs and told the Mounties to expect some bad weather within 24 hours. The policemen courteously listened to his portents, but among themselves shrugged them off as old wives' tale. Macleod did not think to consult his guide and Potts did not think it necessary to reaffirm such an obvious sign. He knew as well as the old trader that they were in for bad weather.

As they took their leave of Akers and Whoop-Up, the four Mounties were again in high spirits. Even if he did still doubt some of the stories about Potts' abilities, he had come to rely on the Metis and trusted him to lead the way in all emergencies. It was a clear but bitingly cold day as they rode south for the Milk River and the campsite at Rocky Springs where Potts had led them to good shelter, wood and grass on their trek north the previous fall.

All day long they travelled through dense herds of buffalo and feeling the excitement of the day and the approaching spring, Macleod forgot about the responsibilities of his position for a short time and decided to test the speed of his horse against that of a buffalo bull. Potts, in his unassuming way, suggested that the colonel would be better off leaving the huge beasts alone. Macleod, in his flashy way, decided to ignore this rather bland warning. Spurring his mount after an old bull he chased it for nearly a mile before catching it. When he did the animal suddenly swung its shaggy head in a savage lunge at his horse. One of the bull's horns caught Macleod's stirrup, ripping away the leather and nearly unseating him as it narrowly missed his leg and his horse's belly.

Managing to keep his seat, Macleod pulled his horse away from the pawing, snorting bull and rejoined his companions. As he rode up, Potts sat slumped in his saddle, his expression knowing but not smug. As Macleod reined up, Potts said: "Colonel, I guess you leave dem ol' buffalo bull alone after dis, hey?"

Since it was near noon they decided to stop and eat while Macleod repaired his stirrup. Potts dug some buffalo chips from under the snow and soon had a campfire going. He told them that they were about half way to Milk River and should reach it by sundown. As they finished eating the sky began to cloud in and it looked as if the bad weather Akers had warned about was moving in. Hurriedly, they packed up and pushed on. With dusk the storm that had threatened all day suddenly unleashed itself with a fury. A stiff, icy wind blew up from the north and as the party reached Milk River they were enveloped in a raging blizzard.

Potts led the men down the steep north bank of the river and told them to unsaddle the horses and stow the saddles and packs under a deep drift close to the cutbank of the river. The cutbank gave them some protection from the whistling wind and swirling snow and the scout told them to take their knives and scoop out a shallow cave in the face of the riverbank. As the men crowded into the shallow hole and huddled together for warmth they asked Potts what to expect. The scout's answer was not very cheering: These late winter storms, he told them, could last for days.

All that night, the blizzard howled and swirled around them. They were to learn later that the temperature dipped to 65 degrees below zero that night. The sudden storm had covered any wood and grass that might have been available so the men had no campfire and the horses no forage. The men slept little if any that night, and when they awoke in the morning the storm was still raging.

With no wood to make a fire they broke out hardtack and used it to push down raw, near frozen bacon that was their only food. During the day a herd of buffalo crowded down the slopes of the riverbank and huddled together in its paltry protection. The storm was so fierce it had driven the usually shy beasts to seek shelter with their usually dreaded enemies, horses and men. The horses, which

NWMP Officers and N.C.O.'s at Fort Macleod in 1874. Standing second from right is Sub-Insp. Francis Dickens, nephew of the novelist Charles Dickens.

the men had picketed on a long rope, bunched up with the shaggy plains animals.

The shallow snow cave they had dug out was now damp and icy cold, and the men were chilled to the bone. They spent a second miserable, sleepless night and with the dawn found the storm as ferocious as ever.

Macleod and the others looked to Potts for direction. The Metis said that the storm could last another couple of days and their supply of bacon and hardtack was almost gone. He told them they had two choices, neither of which the Mounties found particularly heartening: They could stay where they were and die in the snow cave, or try to make it to Rocky Coulee, about 20 miles to the south. There, Potts told them, they would at least find better shelter and, probably, firewood. Macleod decided that this was no time to begin having doubts about the staunch little guide. They would take their chances on the open plains.

Crawling from their cave, the men hauled in the horses and beat the two days of caked ice and snow from their tough hides. The job of saddling and packing with numbed fingers was demanding, but at last they were ready. Setting out on foot and dragging the exhausted, near frozen horses behind them, the NWMP fell in behind their trusted guide.

Taking the lead Potts stayed only a few yards ahead, for any farther and they would have lost sight of him in the blinding snow. The walking brought some life back to their numbed limbs and soon Potts ordered them to mount up. For a while they made better time. They had gone about a quarter of a mile when Inspector Denny noticed that Sub-Constable Ryan was not with them. Hailing the party he rode back a few yards to find Ryan sitting in the snow, holding his horse. Dismounting, Denny crouched beside the man and asked him what was wrong.

"We'll never get through, Mr. Denny," Ryan said. "You and the Colonel go on, I can't make it any farther." Ryan told Denny that he had tried to mount his horse but could not. As he helped the Sub-Constable to his feet Denny saw that his buffalo hide breeches were frozen stiff and the man could not bend his knees. Pushing and shoving he got Ryan into the saddle and led him back to the others.

The storm continued to lash them as they pushed on. Potts plowed on ahead, the policemen following in his tracks, trusting completely in his instincts. "Our guide was a marvel," Denny would say later. "He rode steadily ahead with short stops at intervals when he seemed almost to smell out the trail, for nothing was to be seen in any direction." Towards evening the storm abated a little and ahead the men saw a deep gash in the prairie. Minutes later they rode directly down into Rocky Coulee, the spot Potts had been headed for. There, they spent another hungry, fireless and miserable night, but the shelter was better than it had been at Milk River.

Potts, Macleod, Denny and Ryan crammed together under their buffalo robes for warmth while Sergeant Cochrane huddled among the horses a few yards away. During the night Denny wanted to get up and relieve the Sergeant, but Macleod stopped him saying that if he moved, the snow covering them would fall into their relatively dry bed.

By morning the blizzard had almost blown itself out and the men awoke from their fitful sleep to almost clear skies. The temperature was still very low, but at least they could see where they were going. Sergeant Cochrane and the horses were completely blanketed with snow, but the burly non-com said he had been warm and comfortable throughout the night. Potts advised them against lingering and they headed out on empty stomachs, again leading their emaciated horses.

Potts said they would head for the Marias River where the U.S. Cavalry had an outpost positioned to watch for whisky traders heading for the Canadian border. It was early afternoon when they reached the bank of the Marias and saw the rough shacks of the cavalry outpost. Once again, Potts had come through right on the money.

From their shack the American soldiers saw the five riders spur their horses down the riverbank and, thinking they were smugglers, rode out to intercept them. When they discovered their mistake, Captain Williams invited the sorry looking Mounties into his cabin to be warmed and fed a hot meal of buffalo steaks and steaming tea.

The Canadians then reflected on their ordeal. Although all of them had suffered frostbite to one degree or another, they were in fairly good shape. Extolling the skill of their guide, the NWMP were dumbfounded to learn that Potts had been snowblind during the last miles of their trek to Rocky Coulee. In spite of this he had led them to the exact spot he had intended. Never again would he doubt the abilities of his tight-lipped scout. As far as the NWMP were concerned, Potts' capabilities would never again be questioned. From that day on his skill as a pathfinder became legendary.

After spending a comfortable night with the Americans the Mounties awoke the next day refreshed and eager to continue their journey. Their horses were completely spent so Captain Williams supplied them fresh mounts, a sleigh to carry their baggage, and two men as escort to Fort Shaw. The fort was only 20 miles away and they arrived there early that afternoon.

Fort Shaw was the largest American Army post in Montana territory. Some 400 men manned the post, both cavalry and infantry, under the command of General Gibbon, an old Civil War veteran with many years of service in the Indian wars in the American northwest. Gibbon offered the Canadians the best he had to offer and after two days' rest the visitors were ready to go on to Helena. With an escort and transport supplied by the General, the Mounties continued on to the territorial capital.

Helena was nestled in a picturesque valley in the heart of the Rocky Mountains. A thriving mining town, it had a population of 3,000, most of whom still placer mined in the gulches around the town. The site had been settled in 1856 when a group of down and out prospectors had decided to give it one last try; their dramatic change of luck inspired them to name their strike Last Chance Gulch. The name was considered too vulgar for a territorial capital when business interests in the area were looking for a large town from which to operate, so in 1864 its name was changed to Helena.

Helena, Montana, was a thriving mining town in 1875 when Colonel Macleod and Potts rode there through a blinding blizzard to try and extradict the perpetrators of the Cypress Hills Massacre. Sheriff Healy demanded an exorbitant amount of money for his co-operation and the Mounties rode home empty-handed.

The Mounties found that Irvine had not yet arrived, so Macleod decided to wait for him and send the others back to Alberta. After buying horses, wagons and supplies, Macleod instructed Potts to take the others back to Fort Macleod.

The return trip for Potts and the three Mounties was pleasant and uneventful, their only hardships crossing of swollen, icy streams and rivers. Potts had only been back about a week when Macleod returned from Montana. The colonel stayed only a few days then left for Montana again. There had been a change in plans: Irvine was not going to Helena after all. Instead he had decided to take the train as far as Corrin, Montana then catch a riverboat up the Missouri to Benton. Their difficult and dangerous trek through the blizzard to Helena had been for nothing.

Towards the end of March Potts was instructed to guide Insp. James M. Walsh and a detachment to the Cypress Hills where the police planned to construct another fort. Since the NWMP had arrived in Whoop-Up country, they had had great success in curtailing the whisky traffic. The traders had moved east to the Saskatchewan country where they could carry on their illicit business undisturbed. The Cypress Hills were a rendezvous point for the various Indian tribes during their seasonal buffalo hunts where they could find shelter, water, wood, fresh game, and pasture.

Walsh was a NWMP original. An unassuming man, the inspector was slight of build but rugged in a wiry sort of way. He was sometimes hot-tempered, but could always be counted on to be cool-headed when the chips were down. He was experienced and dedicated and Macleod felt confident he could handle the difficult work that lay in store for him.

Nicknamed "Bub" by his friends, Walsh was one of the most flamboyant and controversial figures ever to ride onto the Canadian plains. His position as a NWMP officer made his actions all the more vexing to his superiors in Ottawa, but Walsh was a man who cared little for bureaucratic authority, and it was this disdain of his unknowing superiors that was to mark his volatile career with confrontation and bitterness.

Walsh was born the first of nine children to a ship's carpenter in the town of Prescott, on the St. Lawrence River, in 1840. Although he was a great athlete, he was a sorry student, and his parents despaired of him ever making very much of himself. When his lack of scholastic progress convinced him to quit school he tried his hand at a variety of jobs from railroad hand to exchange broker. But none of these vocations seemed suited to his latent talents.

By 1866 he thought he had finally found his niche in the world. After graduating from the Kingston Military school with the highest honors in gunnery and cavalry classes, he had assured himself of a commission as major in the regular forces. In 1870 he married 19-year-old Mary Elizabeth Mowat and soon was a father as well as a husband. But the staid life of the civilized east was not for him. He craved adventure and challenge, and in 1873 he saw his chance to seek it.

That year, when the NWMP were looking for recruits, he became one of the first volunteers. Being a major, he was given the rank of Superintendent in the new force and sent on the rounds of Ontario to recruit 50 men of "sound constitution, able to ride, active and able bodied." He knew the caliber of men he wanted and soon had his quota. They in turn soon knew the caliber of their commanding officer.

Their medium height, slight, dark moustachioed Superintendent was, they found, demanding, fastidious, stubborn, impatient and abusive. But he was also fair. When the force marched west to the

Maj. James Morrow Walsh, founder of Fort Walsh and warden over Sitting Bull's Sioux.

plains Walsh showed the qualities of leadership that the fledgling force needed. The difficult march sorely tried the obedience of the men, and it was due largely to officers like Walsh who showed that they could discipline the troopers that the march was a success.

As soon as they arrived in the northwest Walsh was given the special assignment of taking winded stock to the Sun River country of Montana for the winter. On May 12, 1875 Walsh was ordered to take "B" troop, consisting of 75 men, proceed to the Cypress Hills and establish an eastern outpost. Potts was sent along as guide and to help in locating a suitable site for the fort.

After three weeks travel, "B" troop reached Battle Creek in the western slopes of the hills. After a scouting of the nearby countryside, Potts recommended that the fort be established on the creek on almost the exact site of the Cypress Hills Massacre.

The policemen had barely finished setting up their temporary camp of white canvas tents when they had their first visitors. A large band of Indians rode in from the south two days after the Mounties arrived. Potts identified them to Walsh as Teton Sioux and therefore possible trouble. The Major, as Walsh liked to be called, straightened his red tunic and sat down at his table outside his field tent to receive the visitors. Potts warned him that the Sioux were probably hostiles chased across the border by U.S. Cavalry, and to be prepared for trouble.

When the Indians reined up in front of Walsh they showed surprise at being met by soldiers. For generations the Cypress Hills were considered by the Indians to be a sort of no-man's land. After getting over their initial surprise the Sioux offered the Mounties greetings, but suddenly the cordial meeting grew tense. Some of the younger braves noticed that a few of the policemen were wearing the blue jackets and yellow striped pants of the U.S. Cavalry. There were murmurs that the Redcoats were really Longknives who were trying to trick them. Walsh explained that the American clothes had been bought from traders because the men's own uniforms had worn out.

The wary Sioux were not satisfied with the NWMP explanation and accused him and his men of being Bluecoats in disguise. Through Potts, Walsh tried to explain that the flag flying behind him was the Union Jack, the flag of the great grandmother, and not the bluecoated longknives of the great white father.

The Indians still were not convinced and they became increasingly agitated. They pressed around Walsh and Potts, threatening to wipe out the camp. Most of the policemen were out cutting and hauling wood, but the excitement in the camp brought them running with their rifles and ammunition belts. As the NWMP crowded around their commander the Sioux rallied behind their leader.

"If you try to kill us," Walsh warned, "you will lose many of your own and soon there will be more Redcoats here than there are buffalo and none of you will be left alive."

A few tense moments lingered as Sioux and NWMP eyed each other across levelled rifles. Then a band of Cree, friendly to the police, were sighted riding for the camp from the east. Hearing that their hereditary enemies were approaching, the Sioux quickly withdrew. Walsh's first meeting with the Sioux was to be a harbinger of future encounters: over the next several years the Sioux were to be a menacing and troublesome preoccupation for him.

Six weeks after the NWMP arrived in the Cypress Hills, Fort Walsh was completed. While the post was being constructed Walsh and his detachment, with the invaluable help of Potts, succeeded in stamping out much of the whisky trading, thieving, and killing that had been a way of life in the hills for years. Walsh was also successful in getting the Indians of the area to cease their perpetual intertribal warfare. Like Macleod had done in Blackfoot country, Walsh gained the confidence and trust of the tribes and convinced them that their law applied to all men.

Having gained their respect, he then tried to get the tribes together for a council. He sent Potts to the camps of the Bloods and Piegans in the area to ask them to attend the conference. Again the Metis' powers of persuasion were effective. On July 1, the Piegans, Bloods, Crees, Assiniboines and Sioux gathered at a site about 20 miles west of the Cypress Hills to listen to the Redcoat chief's words.

Walsh told them that he had been sent by the great grandmother to etablish law and order, a law and order that meant no cheating or stealing or warfare between the tribes. He impressed upon them that he would always side with those who obeyed the law and would do his best to deal with all the tribes honorably. Pipes were passed and smoked to seal the words of friendship between the tribes, and by the time the council had broken up it seemed that Walsh had had as much success in the Cypress Hills as Macleod had had in the Whoop-Up country. The task he had been given was an enormous one but slowly he succeeded in stamping out the trade in whisky and in stopping the incessant warfare between the tribes.

In 1877 Sitting Bull and the Sioux crossed the line and Walsh was faced with a new challenge. All of the Canadian tribes were enemies of the American Indians and it took all of Walsh's tact and diplomacy to prevent a full-scale war between them. The warlike Sioux were fresh from the Custer battle and spoiling for a fight. Walsh was never a man to back down from one. He was not intimidated by Sitting Bull's reputation or threats and once, when the Sioux chief challenged him, his impatience took over and he physically threw the chief out of his headquarters. When the chief stumbled in the dust Walsh's boiling temper could not resist kicking him in the butt.

Although sometimes strained—at times dangerously so as Sioux and Mounties lined up facing each other with cocked rifles—relations between Sitting Bull and Walsh were good. The Sioux chief saw the Mountie as a man who could be trusted. Walsh, in his romantic way, showed sympathy for the Sioux and their plight; so much so that he was accused of being responsible for Sitting Bull's refusal to return to the United States.

Prime Minister MacDonald was so sure of this that he wrote the Governor-General of the Northwest Territories: "When all this is over I think we must dispense with his services in the Mounted Police." Dispensed with he was in 1883, when Walsh was forced to retire from the force. But being banished from the ranks of the NWMP did not mean that Walsh was about to pine away in oblivion. He became a partner in the Bell, Lewis and Yates Coal Company in Winnipeg, acting as their man in the field at Coal Banks (Lethbridge) in Alberta. Later he became the manager of the growing Dominion Coal, Coke and Transportation Company. In 1897 he was appointed Commissioner of the Yukon with far reaching powers to change mining regulations, hire and fire government officials and—ironically—take full command of the NWMP forces sent north to deal with the lawlessness expected to accompany the Klondike gold rush.

But again he fell into disfavor as he contested government authority just as he had done 20 years earlier. This time he retired voluntarily, leaving the Yukon in a huff in 1899. He retreated to Brockville, Ontario where he spent the next six years growing plump and invectively infuriating. He died in 1906 unnoticed and only incidentally mourned, buried with merely a courtesy salute from the local militia.

☆   ☆   ☆

While the police settled into their new fort, Potts settled into his new home. He pitched his teepee on the prairie nearby and lived with his wives, family and relatives who had accompanied him from Fort Macleod. As the accepted leader of the band he had little to do as his wives attended to his horse herd, leaving him to attend to the NWMP. While he was living more in the world of the whiteman these days, Potts found that the world of the Indian was still very much a part of his life.

One night, as his camp slept, a band of Assiniboines stole in and made off with 35 of his horses. Discovering the theft the next morning, Potts was furious. A few years earlier he would have reacted by loading his Winchester, gathering his relatives and taking out after the thieves. But since he had accepted the presence of the police and their ways of law and order he decided to do it their way.

Fort Belknap, Montana. Potts tracked Assiniboine thieves who had stolen 35 of his horses here in the summer of 1875. Using the ways of law and order he had learned from the Mounties, he recovered his property peacefully.

He went to see Major Walsh and explained what had happened. The Assiniboines, he said, were from across the line and he knew exactly where to find them. He asked Walsh for a letter of introduction to the commander of Fort Belknap in Montana who administered the Assinboine reserve of the same name. He told Walsh that he had seen Indians from that agency skulking around the hills for weeks and now they were gone.

Armed with only a piece of paper, Potts rode south alone. Arriving at Fort Belknap he handed Major Ilges the letter Walsh had given him. Ilges was very accommodating and with a detachment of troops he and Potts rode out to the Assiniboine reserve. There, under the protection of the troops, Potts wandered among the Indian horse herd, picking out the animals that carried his brand. He had 15 of his horses back before the day was out, and by the end of the week he had the other 20.

Thanking Major Ilges for his help, Potts rounded up his herd and headed back to the Cypress Hills, leaving a brooding and bloodlessly couped camp of Assiniboines behind. He had become a true believer in the whiteman's system of justice.

When he arrived back at Fort Walsh he found that the Mounties' newest post was developing as fast as their last one had. The fort had become the nucleus for another town. The I.G. Baker Company had once again followed the police and set up a store, but this time they had competition from the T.C. Powers Company who also were their main competition in Montana. A rustic hotel, laundry, blacksmith shop, billiard hall and several other places of business had also gone up. The town, like the one at Fort Macleod, had been named after the fort. Soon the wide, muddy streets were alive with the hunters, traders, drifters and Indians of the frontier crossroads who were drawn by all the activity in the once quiet hills.

With the fall the police were well settled into their new post and Walsh had acquired the services of a Cree Metis named Louis Leveille to act as his interpreter. The Cypress Hills were in the territory of the Crees and Assiniboines, and the Blackfoot were only summer visitors to the area. So when they returned west for the winter, Potts took his family and horse herd and left for Fort Macleod where his services would be of more value.

CHAPTER EIGHT

Sitting Bull

A T Fort Macleod Potts found that things were going quite well. The post was entirely finished and the NWMP had been well provisioned with supplies and clothing for the coming winter. The tiny town of Macleod had grown too, and its stores were doing a brisk business with the policemen who were at last receiving their pay regularly. The biggest change Potts found was inside the fort. Colonel Macleod, Inspector Winder and Sub-Inspector Shurtliff had brought their wives out from the east; their presence added social grace to the rough frontier outpost.

The scout found other changes, too. The trade in whisky had been all but wiped out. As well as being chief of police, Macleod was also a justice of the peace and as such had full powers to arrest, confine, try and sentence lawbreakers. He was totally confident of his power and enjoyed the authority it gave him. One malefactor sentenced for his whisky peddling fumed and raged, threatening that the telegraph wires to Washington would hum with his complaints. Coolly, Macleod replied, "Let them hum." The colonel was indeed confident of his authority. He once confided to an admirer that he and his Mounties had unlimited power, being able "to try any case and have only to wait for a wink from Ottawa to hang our man."

The most alarming change Potts found was not in the town or the fort but in the nearby plains. Earlier that year some Montanans had brought small herds of cattle north and began an attempt at ranching. Their pioneering venture was a dismal failure as the herds were left to graze on the open prairie and became mixed with the

Sioux chiefs in Saskatchewan: They asked the Blackfoot to join them in their war with the Americans.

buffalo herds. Steers were attacked and gored by the buffalo bulls and the cows were carried off by the dense herds. Still, the idea was alarming to the Metis guide. Two years earlier he would never have imagined that cattle would one day be grazing on the plains of the Blackfoot.

What Potts did not know was that it was the government's intention and the Mounties' job to convince the Indians to become sedentary ranchers rather than nomadic hunters. But the Blackfoot refused to eat beef as long as there were buffalo to be hunted, claiming that to do so was "bad medicine." As Potts looked around his beloved plains he probably agreed with them, but unlike them he realized that it would only be a matter of time before the prairie was empty of wild buffalo and dotted with docile cattle. The plains were truly becoming settled.

Potts resumed his duties as scout and interpreter for the NWMP and during the winter he led patrols and guided the police from one location to another on their everyday tasks. There were few expeditions undertaken in these early years that did not have Potts as a guide. He personally selected and trained men of the force in

(Left) Sitting Bull, the Sioux chief who led his nation in its most concerted effort to drive the whiteman from their ancestral lands in 1876.
(Right) Sitting Bull at Fort Randall, South Dakota, in the winter of 1881-82, getting his first taste of reservation life.

the intricate ways of his trade. Some of the NWMP trained by him became the force's best scouts in later years, two of note being Sub-Inspector Denny and Staff-Sgt. Chris Hilliard.

In June 1876, word reached Fort Macleod of the Custer battle at the Little Big Horn and the war that was raging between the Sioux and the U.S. Army, just a few miles south of the border. At first the NWMP were not too concerned but, early in July, their complacency turned to alarm. When Sub-Inspector Denny was sent to Blackfoot Crossing to arrest an Indian he learned news that put the NWMP on the alert.

The Blackfoot told Denny that the Sioux had recently paid them a visit, asking them to smoke the pipe of peace with them and join in their war against the Americans. They offered the Blackfoot great incentives of captured horses, booty, and even captive white women. The Sioux told them that once they had annihilated the Longknives they would cross over the line and help the Blackfoot destroy the Redcoats. If the Blackfoot did not help them, they threatened, they would cross over the border and destroy them.

When Denny met with Crowfoot the Indians were in a very agitated state. The Blackfoot chief said that he had refused the Sioux request but wanted to know if the police would protect his people if the Sioux rode against them. Denny replied that they would. Satisfied with the policeman's word, Crowfoot then promised that if the Sioux attacked the Redcoats he would send 2,000 warriors against them. Denny did not know it at the time, but by simply giving his word to Crowfoot he was forging a strong pact with the Blackfoot that would make the Indians and the NWMP staunch partners of an alliance that was to be of the utmost importance in the coming years.

The threat of an invasion by the Sioux did not materialize that summer or autumn but, in December, word reached Fort Macleod that 2,000 Sioux with 3,500 horses had crossed the "medicine line" into Canada and camped at Wood Mountain in the Cypress Hills. The Sioux, it turned out, had not come on the offensive, they were in retreat. In May 1877, Sitting Bull himself crossed "the big road" with 135 lodges and camped in the Pinto Horse Buttes east of Fort Walsh. This time the NWMP had something to worry about.

Sitting Bull, the Hunkpapa Sioux chief, is perhaps the most famous of all American Indians. He is best remembered for his defeat of Custer's Seventh Cavalry at the Battle of the Little Big Horn in 1876, but in fact he played only an incidental part in this battle which was probably the Indians' only united and determined effort to rid their country of the whiteman. Sitting Bull was a medicine man, not a warrior, and his fight to preserve his homeland and his way of life was more a spiritual than a physical one.

He was born in 1831 at Grand River in South Dakota, the only son of a Hunkpapa warrior, Returns-Again. At first the Sioux warrior named his son "Slow," for his deliberate and thoughtful ways. One night, while on a raid, a vision told Returns-Again that he was to soon call his son another name. When Slow went off on his first raiding party and returned with his first coup his father changed his name as he had been instructed in his vision. From that day on Slow would be known as "Ta-tan-ka I-yo-ta-ke," the Sitting Bull.

Even in his adolescent years, Sitting Bull was known for his dreams and apparitions and from them acquired his "medicine" which soon identified him in the eyes of his people as a mystic. But he did not spend all his time dreaming. He was a warrior, too. His courage and skill in battle earned him a place in the Strong Hearts Society, an elite warrior group of the Hunkpapa tribe. By the age of 25, he had become its leader. In the mid 1860s he was designated head chief of the Hunkpapas.

The warrior-shaman had no use for the whiteman. When they offered the Sioux nation a treaty and reserve in 1868, he refused to sign, although most of the chiefs did, putting an end to five years of warfare that had come to be known as Red Cloud's war. Sitting Bull and his tribe continued to hunt and live as they always had in the country they claimed as their own.

In 1874 the U.S. Government built a fort in the Black Hills of South Dakota which they felt was necessary to protect the workers who were constructing the Northern Pacific Railroad. The Sioux considered the Black Hills sacred country and harassed the Army for two years. In 1876 Gen. George Crook was ordered into the area to put a stop to the hostilities. One of his subordinates, Gen. George Armstrong Custer, thought that his troop of cavalry could do the job alone.

At the Sioux's annual sun dance that summer, Sitting Bull went through the rigorous ordeal and emerged from it to tell his people that they would soon win a great victory over the Longknives. The Sioux had long ago learned to accept his visions and they mounted their campaign against the whites in alliance with the Cheyennes. The results of the Battle of the Little Big Horn are well known to history.

In its aftermath, the Sioux split into separate camps and scattered across the plains. They were pursued all winter by Crook's forces. Hounded, unable to stop to rest or to hunt the buffalo, Sitting Bull at last sought refuge across the "medicine line" in the great grandmother's country of Canada.

There were some 3,000 hostile Sioux on Canadian soil, fresh from a war with the Americans and still flushed with the victory of the Little Big Horn. They were spoiling for another. The first meetings between Sitting Bull and Major Walsh were tense ones from which the policeman gained shaky assurances from the Sioux chief that he would remain at peace while on Canadian soil.

With each month that the Sioux remained in Canada the tension became greater. All of the Canadian tribes were enemies of the Sioux and they resented the fact that the NWMP were protecting them. They also hated the idea that the Sioux could hunt freely in the hills which they long cherished as their own. The NWMP communicated the news of the tense situation to Ottawa and the usually torpid government became a little unsettled.

Ottawa had two fears, neither of which offered a lesser of two evils solution. Either full-scale war would break out between the Sioux and the Canadian tribes, or the American Indians would bully

Sioux warrior Spotted Eagle, who figured prominently in the Custer battle, was with Sitting Bull at the Fort Walsh peace conference where the Sioux refused to return to the United States.

or cajole Canadian Indians into joining them in a war against the whites. Both were very real possibilities and the normally procrastinating government was goaded into quick action.

A year earlier they had listened to the Blackfoot's promises of peace and co-operation and they moved to reaffirm their handshake agreement. The best way to do that, they thought, was to make legal and binding treaties with the Canadian tribes. In 1876 they had signed a treaty with the Crees and now made plans to ratify one with the Blackfoot.

In September 1877, Colonel Macleod, Commissioner of the force since his appointment in July of the previous year, following the resignation of Commissioner French, received word that David Laird, lieutenant-governor of the Northwest Territories, was coming west to negotiate Treaty Number Seven with the Blackfoot confederacy. Macleod was to have all in readiness for his arrival.

Through Potts, Macleod sent word to all the Blackfoot camps that a great council was to be held at Blackfoot Crossing on the Bow River later that month. Potts impressed upon them they should all be there to hear the words of the white chief. In the following weeks the NWMP prepared the site for the coming negotiations and sent an escort of 108 men north to accompany the lieutenant-governor to the treaty site. By mid-September most of the Indians were assembled at Blackfoot Crossing in the well-timbered valley of the Bow, camped in 1,000 lodges and numbering more than 4,000 people in all.

On September 19, Lieutenant-Governor Laird and Commissioner

Macleod, led by the omnipresent Potts, arrived at Blackfoot Crossing from Battleford in north central Saskatchewan. Two days were spent in explaining just what was taking place, and in haggling between the different chiefs as to just what the treaty would mean. A few times during these parlays it looked as if the negotiations would break down. The biggest factor in the disputes was the petty jealousies between the various tribes and their chiefs, and the constant bickering between individuals as to who should speak for them. Potts' help in ironing out these differences was invaluable. Finally, on September 21, the chiefs met Laird and Macleod to hear the terms and sign the treaty.

Standing by as the lieutenant-governor began his speech of praises and promises was Potts, who had been asked to act as interpreter. When Laird paused and waited for Potts to translate his words, there was only a long silence. Macleod glanced at Potts anxiously and the gruff little scout shifted uneasily on his feet. Looking at Macleod, Potts blurted out his dilemma in typically brief fashion: Laird's speech was so eloquent and articulate, he said, he simply did not understand a damn word the man was saying.

Embarrassed, Macleod hustled Potts out of the limelight. He then quickly found an English half-blood named James Bird, whose loquaciousness, if not his vocabulary, was a little more abundant than Potts'. When the lieutenant-governor had finished speaking, the Blackfoot chiefs rose in turn to have their say.

Red Crow of the Bloods and Bull's Head of the Piegans said that they were willing to accept the terms but, because of Crowfoot's influence among the whole Blackfoot nation, they would leave the final decision up to him. Slowly, regally, Crowfoot rose to speak.

"We are the children of the plains," the chief began; "it is our home, and the buffalo have been our food always. I hope you look upon the Blackfoot as your children now, and that you will be indulgent and charitable to them. They all expect me to speak for them now, and I trust the Great Spirit will put into their breasts to be a good people.

"The advice given me and my people has been very good. If the police had not come to the country where would we all be now? Bad men and whisky were killing us so fast that very few, indeed, of us would have been left today. The police have protected us as the feathers of the bird protect it from the frosts of winter. I wish them all good, and trust that our hearts will increase in goodness from this

Blackfoot Crossing was the scene of the signing of Treaty Number Seven between the Blackfoot Confederacy and the Canadian government in 1877.

Crowfoot speaks to Lieutenant-Governor Laird and the Canadian Commission at the great pow-wow held for the signing of Treaty Number Seven.

time forward. I am satisfied. I will sign the treaty."

With Crowfoot's words the chiefs and headmen of the Blackfoot nation shuffled forward to put their marks to Treaty Number Seven. As the names were recorded on the treaty Potts came to the signing table and spoke with Laird and Macleod, assuring them that the Indians had understood the meaning of the treaty and were sincere in their acceptance of it. He had never in his life, he said, heard them speak their minds so freely.

The ink was hardly dry on the treaty documents when Macleod was informed of another important task he was to undertake, one possibly more important than the signing of the treaty with the Blackfoot. Earlier in the year the American and Canadian governments had held talks to discuss ways of getting Sitting Bull and his Sioux to return to the United States. They had settled on the idea of a U.S. Commission meeting Sitting Bull going in the Cypress Hills and trying to persuade him to return to the States. The Commission, headed by Gen. Alfred Terry, was to arrive at the border in October. Macleod would meet them at the border, south of the Cypress Hills, and escort them to Fort Walsh where the conference would take place. As September was almost over, the commissioner had to make hurried preparations for his trip.

Although Macleod had been embarrassed and angered by Potts' performance at the treaty signing, he asked the Metis to guide him. As it turned out, it was very fortunate that he did.

Potts and Macleod left Blackfoot Crossing with 30 officers and men on September 28 on a journey of over 250 miles, with an unspecified time in which to make it. The first couple of days out they enjoyed fair weather, blue skies and warm temperatures which they expected for this time of year. As they neared the North Saskatchewan River, however, the wind suddenly swung to the north, sweeping in heavy, black clouds. Before they had gone many more miles the police were caught in an early, freak blizzard. On the open plain in unfamiliar country, the NWMP once again found themselves completely dependent upon their guide.

Potts rode out ahead of the column, shoulders hunched, head tucked down as if he were not even looking, and led the way through the tempest. With uncanny skill, he pointed the way southeast. The blizzard lasted four days and each night the scout led them to a suitable campsite with some shelter and plenty of wood for a warming campfire. Each morning he mounted up and headed out in front of the party, riding alone, just within sight of the NWMP.

Macleod said that the Metis reminded him of a centaur, a fantastic half man and half horse who followed some unseen string of guideposts. No one approached the guide as he did the mysterious, almost eerie work of finding the way. The men did not understand the half-blood's skill, but they trusted it and no one dared speak to him for fear that they would break his concentration.

On the fourth day, the savage storm slackened and the NWMP were relieved and amazed to find themselves on a hill overlooking the Battle Creek Valley and Fort Walsh. The incredible Potts had done it again. Macleod was thoroughly convinced. Never again would he doubt or question his guide's skill and competence.

When the NWMP rode into the fort they found that Major Walsh was not there. He had left a few days earlier for Sitting Bull's camp in the Pinto Horse Buttes to try to coax the Sioux chief into coming to Fort Walsh to meet the U.S. Commission. As Macleod awaited Walsh's return, he received word from General Terry that the Commission would be delayed in Benton. Terry's escort had been commandeered to carry supplies to General Miles, who was in pursuit of Chief Joseph's Nez Perce Indians in the Bear Paw Mountains of Montana.

Wanting to use the delay constructively, Macleod set out for Pinto Horse Buttes to meet Walsh and Sitting Bull. With Potts guiding, Macleod's party rode eastward and, two days later, met Major Walsh and Sitting Bull, who was accompanied by about 25 of his sub-chiefs and advisors on the trail. Walsh informed Sitting Bull that Macleod was the head chief of the Redcoats and after the proper introductions and greetings were exchanged the two parties made camp. That evening, Macleod got his first close look at the hostile Sioux and their great chief. But he was a little dismayed to learn that Sitting Bull was adamant about not returning to the United States.

When they reached Fort Walsh the Sioux were reluctant to enter the post but, after assurances from Macleod and Walsh, they agreed to settle down in a tight circle of teepees near its walls. Later that day Macleod received word that the U.S. Commission would be arriving at the border on the 15th of the month.

Terry and his party reached the international boundary late on the afternoon of that day and, through field glasses observed a party of men headed towards them from the north. Their bright red tunics and white pith helmets quickly identified them as NWMP. Ahead of them, leading the way, was a lone, buckskin-fringed and bowler-hatted little horseman.

The next day the Commission and the Sioux met at Fort Walsh. The atmosphere was tense as the Indians and soldiers crowded into the mess hall in the fort. When he entered, Sitting Bull ignored the Americans and walked directly to Macleod and shook hands with him. He offered Terry no handshake or even a word of greeting as he spread a buffalo robe on the floor and sat with his back to the American officials.

Through his interpreter, General Terry explained to Sitting Bull that he had been sent by the President of the United States to offer him and his people peace. If the Sioux returned to the United States they would be granted full pardons. They would be given a reserve and receive food and clothing and would be treated like all other Indians. The only condition was that they give up their guns and horses at the border.

Sitting Bull was not persuaded. He had heard many such promises for 10 years and always they had been broken. Without even glancing at Terry he waved a hand in refusal. Getting to his feet, the Sioux chief gave his answer.

"For 64 years you have kept and treated my people bad," Sitting Bull said. "What have we done that caused us to depart from our country? We could go nowhere, so we have taken refuge here. On this side of the line I first learned to shoot; for that reason I come

Remaining behind in Canada after Sitting Bull returned to the U.S. with most of his people, White Cap was one of the Sioux who joined the Metis in the rebellion of 1885. He is pictured here with his family after his capture.

again; I kept going round and was compelled to leave and come here. I was raised with the Red River half-breeds, and for that reason I shake hands with these people (the Mounties). In this way I was raised. We did not give you our country; you took it from us; see how I live with these people (the police); look at these eyes and ears; you think me a fool; but you are a greater fool than I am; this is a medicine house; you come to tell us stories, and we do not want to hear them; I will not say anymore. I shake hands with these people; that part of the country we came from belonged to us, now we live here."

The Sioux again shook hands with the Mounties and, ignoring the Americans, left the mess hall. Smarting from the abrupt and acrimonious rejection, the U.S. Commission returned home. Terry considered the Sioux to be a Canadian problem and wished Sitting Bull and his recalcitrant cohorts good riddance.

Sitting Bull's remaining years in Canada brought relief from pursuit, but little else. Canadian authorities refused to feed his people, forbade raiding across the border, and the pressures put on the northern buffalo herds by his own large band and the Canadian tribes did not ensure food. When the situation did not improve his people gradually deserted him and returned to the United States until only 185 remained with him. By 1881 he too had enough and he surrendered to the American authorities.

He was held prisoner for two years at Fort Randall until the government, believing him finally broken, allowed him to go to the Standing Rock Agency in North Dakota. By this time enterprising easterners were looking for real live heroes of the Wild West to sell to the public and the "tamed" Indians of the western reserves qualified as prime candidates for their marketable romanticism.

In 1884 Sitting Bull was told that he could go to see the President about the plight of his people if he would agree to go on a tour of eastern cities. Again he was shamefully lied to and was put on exhibit on his tour, billed as the "Slayer of General Custer." A year later, Buffalo Bill Cody talked the Sioux chief into joining his Wild West Show.

Although he allowed himself to be subjected to this form of exploitation he had not forgotten the plight of his people. Two years later, when he heard that the U.S. government was planning to buy out 10 million acres of the Sioux reserve for 50 cents an acre, he became infuriated and fought back. He convinced the other chiefs to flatly reject the offer. But he was fighting a losing battle. The government made another higher offer in 1889, with added inducements such as individual allotments of land for each Indian family. This time the Sioux chief could not convince his fellow chiefs to reject the offer. Asked about the Indians' decision, Sitting Bull replied disgustedly, "Indians! There are no Indians left but me."

Things steadily worsened for the Sioux. Their reserve shrank, their rations were cut, and disease and starvation took a heavy toll. In 1890 a new religion called the Ghost Dance spread north from the Paiute country, promising that the Indians would drive the whites from their country forever and return to the traditional ways of life. Desperate, Sitting Bull became one of its proponents. When frightened white officials tried to stifle the almost fanatical religion by muzzling its leaders, they went after Sitting Bull. His followers resisted. On December 14, 1890 Sitting Bull was shot and killed by a bullet in the head—fired not from the gun of a hated white man, but from the gun of one of his own people who had accepted the ways of the whiteman and rejected those of the Sioux which Sitting Bull had fought for and clung to his entire life.

CHAPTER NINE

Treaty Number Seven

FOLLOWING the failure of the conference between Sitting Bull and the American Commission, Macleod returned to his headquarters with Potts. Shortly after his arrival, a band of Blackfoot under Three Bulls called at the fort to see him. The Commissioner sent for Potts. When the scout arrived, Macleod asked the Blackfoot chief what he wanted.

Three Bulls explained that he and his band had not been present at the signing of the treaty in September. Since then he had seen the benefits his tribesmen were receiving for having put their marks on the paper. He too wanted to share in the whiteman's generosity. Perhaps disgruntled with having to explain the lengthy document to the Indians, or perhaps suffering from one of his particularly bad hangovers, Potts was a little more testy than usual. When Macleod asked him for his interpretation the scout grunted, "He wants grub."

The Blackfoot treaty of 1877, known as Treaty No. 7, was one of the most important documents to be signed between the Canadian Government and native Indian tribes. Not only was it successful in peacefully wresting from the powerful and warlike Blackfoot an area of 35,000 square miles, but it was also important as a pact that would see the Blackfoot remain loyal to the Crown even during the Riel Rebellion of 1885 when their participation in the Metis uprising could have changed the course of Canadian history.

Canadian authorities hurried to conclude the treaty with the Blackfoot confederacy early in 1877 when they learned that the Sioux, who had just crossed the border fresh from the Battle of the

Little Big Horn, were trying to convince the Blackfoot to join them in a war against the whites. In August they sent Lieutenant-Governor Laird to the northwest to complete the treaty. Colonel Macleod was appointed special commissioner for the treaty to act with him. The commissioners had decided on Fort Macleod as the site for the conference but Crowfoot objected to having to go to the

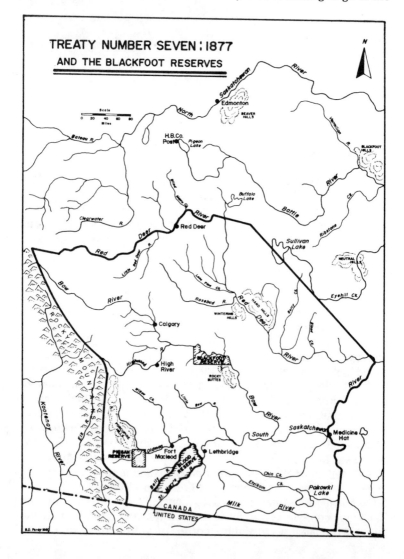

whiteman's fort and demanded that it be held in his territory at Blackfoot Crossing. The Blackfoot chief got his way.

The Bloods and Piegans then threatened to boycott the conference. Macleod and Laird waited for a few days to see if they would come, but Red Crow and his Bloods stubbornly stayed away and the commissioners could wait no longer.

On September 19, the Indians were called to the treaty tent and crowded around the commissioners as the NWMP stood by in their finest red tunics. Lieutenant-Governor Laird read the terms of the treaty explaining that the whites wished to settle on Blackfoot lands. In return for signing the "paper" of permission the Great Grandmother would give them reserves to live on in which each Indian family would be alloted five square miles to live on. They would also be paid 12 dollars per year, the chiefs 25 dollars, and be given yearly rations of beef, flour, farm implements and cattle to begin their own farming and ranching.

In return for these gifts the Indians had to surrender "all their rights, titles and privileges whatsoever to the following lands: Commencing at a point on the International Boundary due south of the western extremity of the Cypress Hills; thence west along the said boundary to the central range of the Rocky Mountains or to the boundary of British Columbia; thence northwesterly along the said boundary to a point due west of the source of the main branch of the Red Deer River; thence southwesterly (sic: southeasterly) and southerly following on the boundaries of the tracts ceded by treaties Numbered Six and Four to the place of commencement."

While the Indians talked over the conditions Red Crow and his Bloods arrived. He had finally changed his mind, feeling that the conference was too important to miss. He also agreed to let Crowfoot speak for him, knowing the Blackfoot chief's talent for diplomacy was greater than his own. Like the other chiefs he would accept Crowfoot's decision.

On Saturday, September 22, Crowfoot went to the Commissioners' tent with Red Crow, Bull's Head, Eagle Tail and other sub-chiefs to sign the treaty. Laird asked them if they had any preference for reserves. The wily Crowfoot immediately asked for his to be set out on his home grounds at Blackfoot Crossing. Eagle Tail and his Piegans wanted a spot of prime real estate in the Porcupine Hills on the Oldman River. Red Crow expressed no interest in having a reserve, but the following year tensions between the Bloods and Blackfoot forced him to take one on the Belly River, southeast of Fort Macleod.

There was no great jubilation among the Indians over signing the

Blackfoot Confederacy Chiefs: Crowfoot of the Siksika (seated left); Red Crow of the Bloods (standing rear); Standing on an Eagle's Tail of the Piegans (seated middle); and Three Bulls of the Blackfoot, were the head chiefs who signed the articles of Treaty Number Seven in 1877.

treaty. Many had not wanted to sign and some of the more militant war chiefs had tried to drum up support against it. The next day the Blackfoot thought they would remind the police that, although they had signed the treaty, they were still lords of their lands and tolerated the whites only because they wished to live in peace with them. That Sunday morning, about 600 Blackfoot warriors, stripped for battle and painted for war, suddenly charged down the hill to the treaty tent and repeatedly circled it while shrilling war cries and firing their rifles into the air.

Laird and Macleod later confided their uneasiness at the Indians' sham battle, saying that any sign of panic on the part of the NWMP could have turned the only half jesting demonstration into a real massacre.

The next three days were spent in paying the Indians the treaty money and impressing upon them what to expect the next year and where to be to receive it. In all some $58,000 was paid out to 4,824 Indians. The police spent the next week watching over the Blackfoot as they spent their first ever money to buy goods from the dozens of traders who had gathered at the site for the occasion. At the end of the week the traders were ordered out and the Indians slowly drifted back to their hunting grounds for the fall buffalo hunt.

It has long been debated whether the Blackfoot really understood what Treaty Number Seven meant. Many Indians later said they did not, for they could not conceive giving up the land they had owned and roamed for generations. Only Crowfoot had any real understanding of what it meant, and even he, it is believed, did not fully realize what "signing" the paper meant. To him it was a pact of good faith and mutual protection between the Indians and whites. In coming years, however, he would learn that in many cases the paper promises which the whiteman always insisted upon were worth less than the words of honor given between two men and sealed with a handshake.

Colonel Macleod, who had gone east earlier that year, returned to Fort Macleod in the summer and prepared to move to Fort Walsh to assume command of the new force headquarters. The commissioner had come to rely heavily on Potts' skills and experience and asked the Metis if he would move his family to the Cypress Hills. In a way Potts had found, if not a home, at least a place among the NWMP and he agreed to move to the force's new headquarters.

In late summer the buffalo moved eastward, close to the Cypress Hills and out of the traditional hunting grounds of the Blackfoot. The Indians, of course, followed them. As mid-September drew near they were told that they would have to return to their reserves in Alberta to receive their treaty annuities. Gathering his people together, Crowfoot led them to Blackfoot Crossing and Macleod and Potts followed. The Bloods and Piegans refused to go there so Potts had to take the commissioner on to the Belly River to pay the Bloods, then to Fort Macleod to pay the Piegans.

At each location Macleod labored with the lengthy business of making the payments. What took so much time was that the money sent from Ottawa was shipped in sheets of one dollar bills which had to be cut into single bills for the payments. Some of the payments were as much as $40,000 and this meant a lot of cutting for the paymaster. But it was considered necessary because the government found that when the Indians received larger bills they were often cheated by unscrupulous traders who would give them labels from fruit and tomato tins as change.

CHAPTER TEN

The Murder of
Constable Greyburn

THE summer of 1879 had been a restless one on the plains of Saskatchewan. The buffalo herds had left the northern prairies altogether, never to return. Hemmed in on the north by the great numbers of Indians which included Sitting Bull's Sioux, the herds had retreated to the Judith Basin area of Montana. With the approach of autumn many of the Indians were near starvation and their horses were too weak to make the long journey south. Those that did manage to make it across the border were rounded up by the U.S. Army and returned to Canada.

Horse stealing was very troublesome, too. Indian raids across the border were numerous and the NWMP were besieged by American stockmen who came north looking to recover their stolen property. Most of the policemen's time was taken up with scouts and patrols to prevent the thefts or restore stolen stock to its owners. Cattle rustling also became a problem as the starving Indians began to prey on the meat only a few years ago they had considered to be "bad medicine."

With so much territory to cover, so many Indians to watch and spread as thin as they were, it was inevitable that sooner or later the police themselves would become victims of the violent and restless times. In November 1879, the NWMP lost their first member to the lawlessness they were attempting to curb.

On November 17, a young, well-liked constable named Greyburn became victim of a murder that to this day has never really been solved. Greyburn, along with three other constables and a sergeant,

(Above) Fort Walsh in 1878 had become the headquarters of the NWMP owing to the tensions on the Saskatchewan plains because of the presence of the Sioux. Unable to be accommodated in the fort, the additional troops had to live in tent camps around it.
(Below) NWMP officers at Fort Walsh in 1879. Colonel Macleod, then the new commissioner of the force, is seated in the chair in the middle.

were on duty in charge of Fort Walsh's horse herd which was picketed about three miles from the post. With all the horse stealing of recent months the NWMP found it necessary to carefully guard their own stock. During the day several men were always on duty and at night the horses were driven into the fort and stabled.

On the day that Greyburn was murdered a small party of Bloods were camped not far from the police herd. In recent days this group had been particularly troublesome, hanging around the fort, begging and making a general nuisance of themselves. When the police guard herded up the horses for their return to the fort they had gone only a mile or so when it was discovered that a picket rope and axe had been left behind. Greyburn cheerfully volunteered to go back and get them. He did not return.

A small search party was sent out to look for him but, because of darkness, they were soon forced to return to the fort. The next morning a larger party was sent out under the direction of Jerry Potts.

During the night a light snow had fallen, completely covering any tracks. From the area of the horse camp Potts moved slowly along the trail, his sharp eyes glued to the seemingly untelling ground. To the others there was not a thing to see but they were about to get another lesson from the inexhaustible repertoire of the plainsman's skills.

Potts suddenly swung his horse off the trail and down a slope into a narrow ravine. The hooves of his horse kicked up a dark patch in the snow. Dismounting, Potts examined the blotch and found it be dried blood. Moving on down the ravine he found Greyburn's pillbox hat, hanging from the branch of a tree. A little farther on, tossed up in the shadows of the gully, was Greyburn's body. The constable had been shot once in the back. Nearby Potts found the policeman's horse tied to a tree and dead from a bullet in the head.

As the NWMP gathered around their slain comrade, Potts reconstructed the murder for them. After riding the short distance back to the horse camp, the scout said, Greyburn was met by two Indians who pulled in beside him and rode along with him. After riding a short while one of the Indians fell behind the Mountie and shot him in the back. The killers then led the horse with Greyburn's body into the ravine, dumped the corpse, tied the horse to a tree and shot it. He was at a loss to explain the motive. Obviously the killers were not after the Mountie's horse, and the men could think of no one who would have had a grudge against the amiable young policeman.

Potts then led the search party to the open plains where he began

On the wild and dangerous plains of Saskatchewan, many of the NWMP troopers preferred the more practical and serviceable buckskins of the frontiersman for the plains over the red tunic and pith helmet of the Mounties.

to track the pair of killers. Before they had gone too far a fall chinook sprang up from the hills, melting the snow and leaving the ground bare and thawed with no clues for Potts to follow.

The murder remained a mystery throughout the winter of 1879-80. Then, in the spring, two Bloods from a camp near the fort were arrested for horse stealing. There was no direct link between them and the Greyburn killings, but whisperings in the Indian camps said that the two were to be tried for the murder of the policeman. The two prisoners soon heard the rumors and began to fear for their lives.

Together they planned a break for freedom. When they were taken outside the fort for an exercise period one day, they waited for their guards to relax their vigilance, then made their break. The police guards, in their awkward riding boots, were no match for the fleet-footed, moccasined Indians. The alarm was given and a few Mounties were quickly mounted and in hot pursuit.

As the fugitives reached their camp they were met by their wives who handed them their rifles and ammunition belts. The two

Indians were out on the open prairie when they were overtaken by the NWMP. At first the Bloods stood their ground and faced the Mounties over levelled rifles. But as the police encircled them with their own weapons aimed, they gave up without a fight. Back in the stockade at Fort Walsh, the Bloods decided to talk rather than face what they thought would be a murder charge.

At midnight they sent word to Major Crozier, commanding the post in Macleod's absence, that they wanted to talk to him. They said that they had information about the Greyburn murder but would only give it to him secretly in his quarters. To ensure secrecy they said, Crozier should cover the windows of his quarters with blankets so no one could observe them from outside. Crozier agreed and, around midnight, had the two Bloods smuggled to his cabin.

The Indians gave Crozier the description and name of the Indian they said had killed Greyburn. His name was Star Child and he was hiding out in the remote recesses of the Bear Paw Mountains in Montana. Crozier knew Star Child and his reputation as a troublemaker. Feeling that the prisoners had no reason to lie he decided to investigate further.

He sent a telegraph to Colonel Macleod, who was in Benton on his return to the Cypress Hills. The commissioner had been east to see about getting an appointment as a stipendary magistrate for the Macleod district of Alberta. He had recently decided to retire from the NWMP.

When he received Crozier's wire, Macleod went to see the sheriff of Benton to ask his help in capturing Star Child. Fate could not have played a more ironic trick on him. The sheriff of Benton was John Healy of the old whisky trading days of Whoop-Up country, whose lucrative trade with the Indians had been pinched off by the Mounties six years earlier. Healy never did forgive the NWMP and when Macleod went to him with his request he said he would help if Macleod paid him $5,000. Macleod interpreted this was tantamount to blackmail and refused the demand as ridiculous. Instead he would wait until Star Child returned to Canada as he undoubtedly would since all his relatives were living near Fort Macleod.

Upon his return to Fort Walsh, Macleod put all in order for his retirement from the force and in late September returned to Fort Macleod to take up his civilian duties. Accompanying him were Cecil Denny who was going on leave, his nephew Donald Macleod, who was going to join his father Norman who had recently been appointed Indian Commissioner to the Blackfoot, two Mounties, and Jerry Potts who was going to rejoin his people on the Piegan reserve in the Porcupine Hills.

At Whoop-Up crossing on the Belly River, Macleod and Potts forded on horseback but, as night was coming on, the colonel advised the others who were riding in the baggage wagon to wait until morning. Potts and Macleod went on to the fort about nine miles away. The next morning Denny and the others were crossing the river when the horses spooked and the wagon overturned in midstream. Denny, Macleod and one of the Mounties made it to shore but the other policeman, Constable Hooley, was drowned.

In the year since their absence from the town of Macleod, Potts and the ex-commissioner found that it had grown even more. The Oldman River had changed its course and was undercutting the fort and the town itself. Huge chunks of the riverbank would periodically fall off into the fast-flowing river, carrying buildings and all with it. Those forced to relocate took advantage of the opportunity to expand their premises.

The surrounding country was showing more signs of settlement, too. There were more and bigger herds of cattle roaming the prairies near the town and the word rancher was becoming as common as whisky trader had been 10 years earlier. The Indians, caught up in the fast changes, were swept along as hapless victims in the flood of white expansion. The Blackfoot had returned empty-handed the previous fall from chasing the buffalo in the Milk River area; throughout the winter and spring, they crowded around the fort, looking for handouts of beef and flour.

Many of the Indians were on the verge of starvation. Some went so far as to eat grass, and the sickest had to be carried to the fort where their relatives begged food for them. Whenever the police shot a steer for them, the starving Indians would rush at it with their butcher knives and hack off chunks of meat from the still kicking animal and gulp them down raw. The whiteman's beef was no longer "bad medicine."

Potts was saddened by the changes he saw in his people. Their proud way of life was gone and they were reduced to a ragged, starving and begging race of scavengers. Their lifestyle was lost—destroyed not by guns, or even the accursed firewater, but by the whiteman's relentless settlement of the land. Fort Macleod was just too crowded for Potts and he went to live on the Piegan reserve.

Although suspected of murdering Constable Greyburn in 1879, Star Child was not convicted of the charge but spent time in a Manitoba jail for horsestealing. Upon his release he returned to Alberta where he enlisted as a scout with the NWMP. He is pictured here holding a Winchester '73 with the long wooden forearm which was the official weapon of the force.

Although shunning the ways and settlements of the whites, Potts still made his services available to the NWMP and never refused their request for help. On one of his visits to Fort Macleod a tragedy occurred that would bring about a disturbing change in the man, although his inscrutable facade would not show it. On October 29, 1880, Potts was at Fort Macleod. While examining the priming of an old fuke, the dilapidated weapon exploded and killed a young child.

It is not known who the child was, perhaps one of his Indian relatives, but after the accident Potts did not seem to be himself anymore. He became more sullen, even morose, and seemed to shun all company, including that of the police except when he was summoned to do a job for them. He withdrew to the isolation of the Piegan reserve where it would appear the bottle became his best and only friend. He still looked upon the Mounties as his employers and the Blackfoot as his people, but no man could ever really call the Metis his friend.

In his movements among the camps of the Bloods and Piegans in the winter of 1880-81, Potts learned a piece of news that would bring the unsolved murder of constable Greyburn to a judicial although inconclusive end. The scout heard that the renegade Star Child was on the Blood reserve but he was difficult to locate because he was constantly on the move. In May Potts finally pinned him down and rode into Fort Macleod to report to Major Crozier.

Crozier sent two corporals and two constables with Potts to make the arrest. The camp where the suspected murderer was hiding was on the banks of the Little Bow River, about 18 miles from Fort Macleod. Potts and the Mounties arrived at the camp just as dawn was breaking and the scout quietly led them to the lodge where the fugitive was sleeping. As they surrounded the teepee some sixth sense alerted Star Child that he was in danger and he emerged from the lodge with his rifle levelled. He pointed the gun at Sergeant Patterson and threatened to shoot him if he made a move. Using an old ruse Patterson spoke as if to someone behind the Indian. Star Child fell for it and the sergeant pounced on him, driving him to the ground. As they fell, Star Child's rifle discharged, ending the Mounties' hope of taking him without arousing the camp.

In moments the village was awake and dozens of armed Indians gathered around the scene. By then Patterson was on top of Star Child, pinning him in a choke hold as he clamped the handcuffs on him. Potts and the other policemen pulled their six-guns and held the pressing throng of excited braves at bay. As Patterson hauled Star Child to his feet, the Bloods pressed even tighter. They were determined that the police would not take their prisoner. But the

NWMP were just as determined that they would.

Pushing and shoving their way through the ring of riled Indians, the Mounties made it to their horses. Getting Star Child mounted, Patterson raced off to Fort Macleod while Potts and the others followed, all the while holding the furious warriors off at gunpoint. The angry Bloods followed them all the way to Fort Macleod where they were forced to turn back.

Star Child eventually confessed to murdering Constable Greyburn and there was evidence and testimony that seemed to confirm his guilt. But, at his trial, the white jury found him not guilty and, much to the astonishment of Indians and whites alike, he was set free. The jury explained their decision by saying that they believed Star Child had confessed to the murder because he was seeking recognition as a great warrior. It would be very "big medicine" for an Indian to kill a Redcoat, for he would be the first Indian to do so since the NWMP had arrived.

Colonel Macleod, who tried the case as judge, suspected that the real reason for the verdict was based on the jury's own fears. Most of them were cattlemen and feared reprisals from the Bloods if they brought in a guilty verdict.

Just as the furor of the Star Child affair was dying down, Potts was asked to perform another duty. The Governor General of Canada, the Marquis of Lorne, son-in-law of Queen Victoria, was to make a tour of the Northwest Territories and the NWMP were to be escort. The force at Fort Macleod was assigned escort duty from Blackfoot Crossing to Fort Shaw in Montana, where the Marquis would take a train back east. Potts was hired on as official guide and interpreter for the last leg of the tour.

In September the NWMP escort followed Potts north to Blackfoot Crossing. A few days later, the Governor-General arrived with his entourage of wagons and carts, large police escort, and a party of Crees led by Chief Poundmaker who had been the party's guide through Cree country to the northeast. After an official reception, which included gun salutes and inspection of ranks, the Marquis met with Crowfoot and his people in a great conference which was meant to reaffirm the promises made in the treaty of 1877.

With the conference over, the column formed up and headed south. Potts galloped out ahead, riding alone as he always did. After a day or two of travel the Governor-General became curious about the little half-blood who rode out early in the morning and stayed far ahead of the column, never speaking to anyone. On this particular morning he decided to join the scout.

For all the Marquis' importance, Potts was not very impressed. All

Although he worked for the Mounties, Potts remained steadfastly loyal to his people and their way of life. Pictured here (standing at right of Indian standing center) at the Blood Sun Dance in the 1880s, he showed that the Blackfoot were his first people.

the fuss and ceremony probably irked him a little and he never had been a lover of flowery vocabulary. As Lord Lorne reined up beside the scout, he said politely; "Hello Jerry." Potts did not even acknowledge him. Riding on a little way the Marquis tried again to draw the tight-lipped Metis into conversation. "I say, Jerry," the Governor-General said, "After we pass that hill up ahead there, what do we come to?" Again Potts ignored him, staring silently ahead at the course he was steering.

The Marquis repeated his question and when it still brought no reply he snapped, "I say, Jerry, don't you hear me? After we pass that hill what do we come to?" Potts, a little miffed by all this conversation, levelled a black-eyed, piercing scowl at the Governor-General and grunted, "Nudder hill, ya damn fool."

Potts' surly mood continued throughout the trip. He had always been naturally close-mouthed but he was also known to be mild-tempered. When the cavalcade reached the Piegan reserve in

Montana they camped for the night near the trading post of two men named Hamilton and Hazlett. With the approach of evening Potts rode into the trading post and bought himself a crock of red-eye.

Soon after he returned to camp he had one leg well in the bag. Earlier in the day he had seen an old Piegan chief with whom he had a long standing grievance, and decided it was time to settle the score. The NWMP who were drinking with the scout tried to discourage him from going after the old Indian. The police, of course, could not allow anything to happen that could create an international incident, and the killing of a reserve Indian on American soil by Canadian police would certainly qualify as such.

Potts could not be dissuaded, however. He insisted on settling the grudge and went for his rifle. The police had to physically restrain him and in the scuffle his rifle went off, the bullet narrowly missing one of the constables. It took considerable force to wrest the gun away from him and once he was disarmed he had to be tied up and guarded throughout the night.

It was not just the Marquis of Lorne's tour that seemed to be troubling the tenacious scout. Even after his return to Fort Macleod his untypically irresponsible behaviour continued. When a report reached the fort that two American traders with a wagonload of whisky had crossed the border, Potts was sent with two constables to arrest them. The scout led the policemen to a spot on the St. Mary's River where he knew they would have to cross. Hiding in the brush they waited for the wagon to appear. Later that evening the wagon came rolling down the riverbank and right into the waiting arms of the scout and policemen.

The two smugglers were handcuffed together and placed in the back of the wagon with their wares. Potts volunteered to guard them so one of the Mounties took the reins while the other took charge of the saddle horses. Whether he knew the two traders from his days in Fort Benton, or just struck up a conversation with them—which is very unlikely—Potts soon had the barrel of firewater unplugged and was sampling its quality. Not a man to drink alone, he asked the two peddlers to join him. By the time they reached Fort Macleod, Potts and the prisoners had drunk themselves unconscious. The whisky was gone and, with it, the evidence.

These episodes and others sorely tried the patience of the scout's NWMP employers and were explained away by some as Pott's unashamed love of the pure. As one Mountie said, "Potts had an unquenchable thirst which a camel might have envied. He drank whiskey when he could get it. If he could not get it, he would take

Jamaica ginger, or essence of lemon, or Perry Davis' painkiller, or even red ink."

Yet Potts was not alone in having "an unquenchable thirst." Most men of this frontier time were indulgers. Indeed, some of the most flagrant abusers of the prohibition laws were the NWMP themselves. In a time and place where isolation and boredom were eternal curses, men looked to the only thing—fancied or real—that brought them any kind of relief or solace, the bottle. Although Potts had always been known as a drinker, his latest antics tried even the patience of the police.

As Dempsey put it: "Everyone who knew Potts admitted he was an unusual man and felt that his drinking was not uncommon on the frontier. With his virtues far outweighing his sins, he was considered to be a capable scout, guide and interpreter rather than just a drinker. Regardless of his condition, no one could question his honesty, bravery and faithfulness to the Mounted Police." Last of all to question Potts' faithfulness to the NWMP were the police themselves.

CHAPTER ELEVEN

The Riel Rebellion

THE day after New Year 1882, trouble broke out on Crowfoot's reserve at Blackfoot Crossing. Since the disappearance of the buffalo the Indians had been relying on their treaty annuities to supply their winter rations. Over the last couple of years the rations had been greatly reduced and resentment of the agency officials had degenerated into bitterness.

On January 3, while the Indians were receiving their allotments, a sub-chief named Bull Elk was treated curtly by agency employees when he tried to buy a steer's head. He went away angry and returned with his rifle. He fired two shots at the agency building, one hitting the logs not far from where one of the employees was working.

When the Indian Agent complained to Fort Macleod, Inspector Dickens and two constables were sent to arrest Bull Elk. Upon the Mounties' arrival at the Crossing, they found the Indians in a very excited state. Searching out Bull Elk, Dickens place him under arrest and began to lead him to the agency building. The throng of Indians became enraged and pressed around the policemen, pushing and shoving and firing their guns into the air. More and more armed Indians arrived by the minute and some blocked off the trail leading from the agency. The Blackfoot were determined that, this time, the NWMP would not get their man.

Dickens anxiously sent for Crowfoot, hoping he could defuse the tense situation. As the inspector and the two policemen tried to drag their prisoner into the agency building, there was a scuffle and

Dickens was knocked to the ground. Getting to his feet he pulled his pistol and the pressing Indians withdrew slightly—enough for the constables to get the prisoner inside. By the time Bull Elk had been dragged inside the agency building there were almost 200 armed warriors gathered outside, screaming and taunting as they fired their guns into the air in an attempt to provoke the Mounties into firing at them.

When Crowfoot arrived, he demanded that Bull Elk be released. The chief was in an ugly mood and adamant in his conviction that Bull Elk was not guilty of anything and should be set free. Dickens refused to release Bull Elk, saying that he must go to Fort Macleod for a trial. Crowfoot said that he would not let them leave with the prisoner.

After much discussion a compromise was struck. Crowfoot promised that if Bull Elk was released in his custody he would guarantee his appearance for trial when summoned. Under the circumstances, Dickens agreed.

The inspector then sent word to Fort Macleod and, the next day, Superintendent Crozier and 20 men guided by Potts set out for Blackfoot Crossing. Once there, Crozier immediately sent for Bull Elk who obediently appeared, knowing that there was a large force of police on the reserve. In the agency building Crozier began an on-the-spot inquiry into the incident. Through Potts he got the Indian side of the affair, then listened to the agency employees. He decided that Bull Elk would have to return to Fort Macleod for trial.

While he questioned the witnesses, Crozier had the agency building fortified with breastworks made from sacks of flour and oats. When Crowfoot heard of this, he appeared at the agency with a large party of armed braves. Impressed with the preparations Crozier had made, the chief asked him if he intended to fight. "Certainly not," Crozier replied, "unless you commence."

Crowfoot again asked that Bull Elk be remanded to his custody but Crozier flatly refused. The rifle-wielding police remained overnight with an armed guard on duty, then left in the morning with their prisoner tightly encircled. At Fort Macleod Bull Elk was tried before Magistrate Macleod and sentenced to 14 days in the guardhouse. The sentence was light because Macleod did not want to further complicate an already dangerous situation. He later confided: "It has been a nasty business."

The incident proved that the NWMP still needed their tough Metis scout and interpreter. It was as much due to Potts' powers of persuasion as it was to Crozier's courage that the confrontation at Blackfoot Crossing had not turned into a bloody shootout. Even though the scout continued to prefer the buffalo-skinned lodges of the Indian camps to the wooden buildings of the whiteman's towns, he remained loyal to the police. The NWMP recognized that he was not just another employee. They had long since become convinced of his great influence among the Blackfoot. If any trace of doubt remained about his stature among the Indians or his loyalty to the

Louis Riel, the Metis leader of the Northwest Rebellion of 1885.

War leader of Riel's Metis, Gabriel Dumont escaped capture at Batoche but was later apprehended by the U.S. Army at Fort Assiniboine.

police, they were forever put to rest in the summer of 1885.

In March 1885 the flames of rebellion that had flared 15 years earlier on the Canadian plains and smoldered ever since erupted into a conflagration that engulfed the whole Dominion of Canada and threatened to tear it asunder. After the Red River Rebellion of 1869 the Cree Metis who had fled to the plains of Saskatchewan to be clear of encroaching settlement again found themselves having to fight to protect their lands and their rights.

As the railway pushed westward and the white settlers followed it, the Canadian government threatened to seize their traditional hunting grounds and claim them as Crown lands. They would then offer to grant them to the Metis, but only after they had been surveyed and deeded. The surveyors wanted to lay the tracts out in large blocks, but the Metis argued that they should be laid out in long strips along the rivers so that every man would have access to water. The government ignored their requests and the Metis had no one to appeal to. If they were going to have any rights they knew they would have to fight for them.

In June 1884, four Metis hunters rode south to St. Peter's, Montana to call on their exiled leader, Louis Riel, who had been teaching school there since his flight in 1869. Riel was not sought out to lead the Metis in battle, the man who rode at the head of the four horsemen would do that. He was Gabriel Dumont, a noted horseman, rifleman and leader of the buffalo hunts. He would be the military commander but he had no gift for arousing and uniting the Metis under him. Riel did.

Dumont convinced the French Metis to come back to the Saskatchewan plains with him and again take up the cause of their people. Riel, who claimed to have had visitations from God, believed that he had a mission in life and that the time had come to fulfill it. A few days later, he rode north with his family and the Metis messengers to Saskatchewan.

Riel and Dumont went to Batoche, the chief Metis settlement of the northwest on the South Saskatchewan River. There, the Indians were in a very restless mood. The three tribes of the confederacy were being handled by three different agents, each with his own ideas about how the Indians should be treated. Rations had been cut in half, supplies were often late in arriving, and stories of the Crees and their uprising had the Blackfoot in an anxious state.

In March, 1885, after Ottawa ignored the bill of rights he had drafted, Riel announced that he was taking up arms to win the rights he had petitioned for. The strategy he decided upon was to be a repeat of the one he had followed in the Red River Rebellion. He set up a provisional government and formed an "army" of about 400 Metis cavalry under command of Gabriel Dumont. Telegraph lines were cut, government agencies seized and several hostages taken.

Riel then demanded the surrender of Fort Carlton, the closest bastion of government forces where Insp. Lief Crozier and 50 Mounties were stationed. Crozier's answer was to march on one of

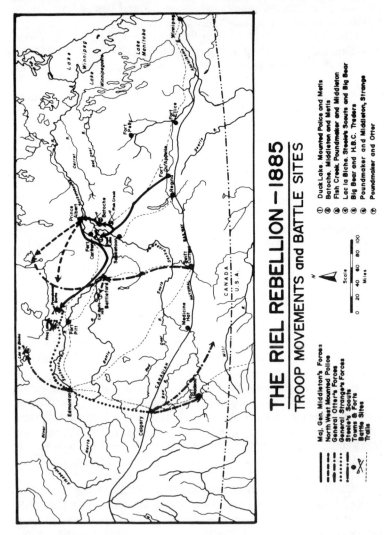

THE RIEL REBELLION – 1885
TROOP MOVEMENTS and BATTLE SITES

Maj. Gen. Middleton's Forces
North West Mounted Police
General Otter's Forces
General Strange's Forces
Steele's Scouts
Towns & Forts
Battle Sites
Trails

① Duck Lake. Mounted Police and Metis
② Batoche. Middleton and Metis
③ Fish Creek. Poundmaker and Middleton
④ Lac la Biche. Steele's Scouts and Big Bear
⑤ Big Bear and H.B.C. Traders
⑥ Poundmaker and Middleton, Strange
⑦ Poundmaker and Otter

Riel's strongholds at Duck Lake. The NWMP got a lesson in the type of guerrilla warfare the Indians and Metis could wage. On March 26 Dumont's Metis ambushed Crozier's force in a narrow gully. Ten of the Mounties were killed and 14 wounded before Crozier could manage a difficult retreat.

Word of the rebellion spread quickly. Crozier evacuated Fort Carlton and sent word into the surrounding country for all civilians to gather at Prince Albert, which he planned to fortify against attack. From Regina to Ottawa, the telegraph wires hummed. Troops were mobilized and hastened aboard special non-stop trips to the northwest.

A few days after the Duck Lake battle, Riel sent word to the Crees asking them to join the rebellion with a full-scale uprising. Two of the Cree chiefs agreed, each for different reasons. Poundmaker, the adopted son of Crowfoot, hated reservation life and Big Bear ruled over a bunch of malcontents who hated whites. Poundmaker led his forces to Battleford where some 500 civilians had crowded into the small NWMP post there for protection. The Crees ransacked the town and laid siege to the fort for three weeks before they tired of the wait and went in search of easier prey. Farther north, Big Bear led his braves to the Hudson's Bay Company post at Frog Lake where they massacred nine civilians, including two priests.

In Blackfoot country things remained quiet on the surface while beneath, they were smouldering dangerously. The NWMP grew apprehensive over the growing unrest of the Blackfoot tribes and approached Cecil Denny, then ranching in the Macleod area, about becoming Indian Agent for the Blackfoot again. Denny had left the force a couple of years earlier to become Indian Agent but had soon resigned because of government bureaucracy. He was well-liked and respected by the Blackfoot and had treated them fairly. He agreed to take the job on again but only on condition that he have complete authority when dealing with the Indians. The NWMP eagerly complied.

The month after the outbreak of hostilities the new Indian Agent travelled to the camps of the Bloods and Piegans and, with the aid of Potts, learned their gripes and fears first-hand. Their chief complaint was that they did not have enough to eat. Denny immediately doubled their rations of beef and flour and gave them seed grain and potatoes for their farming operations. Dispelling their fears about the Crees and their uprising, he then gained assurances that they would remain peaceful and stay on their reserves. The Blackfoot were so grateful for Denny's treatment that they even volunteered to battle the Crees.

Denny's report to the lieutenant-governor was received with great relief, especially the part about the Blackfoots' offer to go on the warpath against the Crees. On May 1, Denny received a coded telegraph from Lieutenant-Governor Dewdney which surprised, even shocked, the Indian Agent. Dewdney's telegraph read: "A few Crees some thirty in number around Cypress skulking. Would like Blackfoot to clean them out. Could this be done quietly? Advise me before taking action."

Denny could hardly believe his eyes. He could not believe that the government was actually considering setting the Canadian tribes at war with one another again after the NWMP had spent 12 years trying to keep peace among them. He replied that he would not send either the Bloods or the Piegans because all the others would also want to leave their reserves and he would not be able to keep track of them. He felt that this would be a sure way to involve the Blackfoot tribes in the rebellion and it could backfire and have grave consequences for the government.

After the Duck Lake battle there was no turning back for the Metis—the war was on. Within 24 hours of receiving word of the battle, the first troops were dispatched to Fort Qu-Appelle. Command of the army was placed in the hands of Maj.-Gen. Frederick Middleton, who, with two smaller forces under Col. William Otter and Maj.-Gen. Thomas Strange, moved that summer in a three-pronged march from the railroad in the south. Middleton moved on the Metis headquarters at Batoche, Otter was to go to the relief of Battleford, and Strange was to engage Poundmaker's and Big Bear's Crees near Fort Pitt.

Middleton, like Crozier, received a rude lesson in Metis tactics. He was ambushed by Dumont at Fish Creek and in the sharp battle that followed he lost 50 dead and wounded. It took the Major-General two weeks to get over the shock and regroup for another offensive.

General Otter reached Battleford and relieved its inhabitants, than marched on Poundmaker at Cut Knife Hill. He, too, was taught his first lesson in Indian warfare. The Crees saw the approaching Redcoats and slipped out of their village to lay in the brush and watch while Otter's cannons bombarded empty teepes. In half an hour the troops found themselves fighting for their lives. With only 300 warriors armed with poor trade muskets and bows and arrows, Poundmaker soon had Otter's 400 well-armed and trained soldiers on a hasty retreat to Battleford.

Further west, General Strange had enlisted the aid of 25 Mounties under Insp. Sam Steele (they became known as Steele's Scouts) to run Big Bear and his band to ground. Steele's Mounties, long used to

(Left) One of the two leaders of the Crees in the Riel Rebellion, Poundmaker outsmarted and outfought the Canadian forces on several occasions.
(Right) Sir Frederick Dobson Middleton, pictured here in March 1889 on ice skates.

The surrender of Poundmaker to Major-General Middleton at Battleford, Saskatchewan, May 26, 1885.

the Indian ways, had better success than the other forces. They picked up the trail of Big Bear and 200 of his braves and, two days later, engaged the Crees at Frenchman's Butte. After a sharp initial encounter, Strange ordered the attack broken off when it looked as if the Indians would surround him. As he put it, he did not want to "commit another Custer."

Meanwhile, at Batoche, Middleton prepared to attack the Metis stronghold. When he did he was again driven back by Dumont's riflemen. Again he hesitated. Advice given by his officers was ignored until, finally, one of his colonels took the initiative into his own hands. He led a charge on the Metis trenches that swarmed over them by sheer force of numbers. Beaten back from their rifle pits, the Metis fought on from the shelled ruins of Batoche but, by evening, it was all over. The beaten Metis surrendered.

Gabriel Dumont was not among them. He eluded the troops and escaped to Montana where he later became an attraction in Buffalo Bill's Wild West Show. Riel was captured a few days later, hiding in the woods. Middleton took him and the other rebels to Regina for trial.

Up north, Poundmaker had decided to surrender after hearing of the fall of Batoche and gave himself up to Otter at Battleford. Big Bear, after being hounded for two months in the northern woods and boglands, stumbled into Fort Pitt on June 18 and gave himself up. Eleven of the Cree rebels were tried for murder at Battleford and sentenced to hang. Three were granted a reprieve but the others were hanged from a common scaffold. Both Poundmaker and Big Bear were sentenced to serve three years in a Manitoba prison for their parts in the rebellion. They served one year of their terms and were released. They returned to their homelands broken in health and spirit and both died within six months of their release.

As for the visionary Riel, he was tried at Regina for treason and sentenced to death. Plainly, there was no defence for his treason except insanity, which his dignity would not permit him to plead. On November 16, 1885 he was hanged at Regina prison. His body was shipped back to his native Manitoba and buried in Winnipeg under a granite stone which read, simply, "Riel; 16 Novembre, 1885."

Potts' role in convincing the Blackfoot to stay out of the rebellion was probably greater than that of the NWMP. As Dempsey wrote: "Potts' role in helping the Mounted Police and Indian Agents to keep peace among the Bloods and Piegans during the Riel Rebellion was one which brought him praise and honour. Playing on the natural enmity between the Blackfoot and Crees, Potts travelled through

Big Bear, Cree chief, is shown here with his Mountie captors after the unsuccessful Northwest Rebellion of 1885.

the excited camps offering latest news of Cree defeats, disputing wild rumors sent by half-breed messengers, and bolstering the authority of elder chiefs who were counselling for peace. His ability to deal with an explosive situation with diplomacy and tact was of immeasurable value as he went with police officers from camp to camp during the early weeks of the rebellion."

When Riel's short-lived rebellion was crushed later that summer, the threat of a Blackfoot uprising passed, but the symptoms that could have precipitated it persisted.

With the excitement of the past few months behind him, Potts returned to the Piegan reserve in the Porcupine Hills where he soon had a small cattle ranch going. It was not that he was suddenly taken with the whiteman's ways but, unlike his full blood brothers, he had learned that things were about to change even more in the northwest. The rebellion had brought a hurriedly completed railroad to the country. It had doubled the size of the NWMP force from 500 to 1,000 men and there were more soldiers on the plains than ever before. Most importantly, it brought hundreds of settlers streaming into the country on the new iron horse—a tide that could not be stemmed.

However reluctantly, Potts accepted the whiteman's way as the only way to survive. The buffalo were gone and if his family were to eat they had to have beef. He would not steal them so the only alternative he saw was to raise them.

CHAPTER TWELVE

The Last Ten Years

WITH the increase of settlers into the northwest the Blackfoot found new targets for their horse and cattle stealing raids. Their traditional victims, the Montana Gros Ventres and Assiniboines, were not forgotten either. Raids back and forth across the border became even more commonplace and the NWMP knew they had to put a stop to them before they erupted into a bloody war.

Late in 1886, a raiding party of Bloods returning from Montana were ambushed just south of the border by a band of Gros Ventres and all the Bloods were killed. When the news reached the Blood reserve the Indians were furious and threatened to take 400 warriors across the border in the spring to make war on the American tribes.

The Blood Indian Agent, William Pocklington, informed the NWMP of the situation and the police moved quickly to try to head off the war they had been expecting for some time. They knew that they were spread too thin along the border to prevent small raiding parties from crossing freely. What they needed, they realized, was a string of outposts along the border connected by regular patrols that could watch and report on the movements of the Indians to and from the U.S. Such outposts would have to be strategically located and they sent for the man who they knew could do the job.

The following spring, Potts guided the police to well-known border crossings such as Writing-on-Stone, Pendant O'Reille and Milk River Ridge, where the Indians always crossed the line on their raids. Small outposts were set up at these and other locations from which the NWMP could observe any suspicious riders headed to or from the border and intercept any would-be or returning raiding parties. The threatened punitive raid by the Bloods did not take place that summer and over the coming years these outposts were very successful in eliminating Indian raids, whisky smuggling, and horse and cattle rustling.

The winter of 1887 was a devastating one for cattlemen in Alberta, including newcomers like Potts. The previous winter had been a very mild one and most ranchers had failed to put up enough hay. When the savage blizzards hit, whole herds were caught in the open and thousands died. More were lost due to the shortage of feed. That fall, the I.G. Baker Company had brought in the first herd of beef steers to Alberta and lost most of them to the winter. In all, some 25,000 head of cattle were lost in southern Alberta that winter. Nevertheless, Potts knew that cattle would return before the buffalo would.

As the 1880s wore on, Whoop-Up country became more and more settled and so did the Blackfoot. So did Jerry Potts. When his two Piegan wives died he took his fourth and final spouse, "Isum-its-tsee" or Long-Time-Laying-Down. Since his new wife was the daughter of the Blood chief, One Spot, Potts was obliged to follow the Indian custom and return to his own people on the Blood reserve on the Belly River.

Yet, as settled as the country was becoming, there were still exciting and dangerous times ahead for the long-time scout and interpreter who was affectionately known among the NWMP as "Old Jerry." In the summer of 1889, the Bloods were preparing for their annual Sun Dance on the reserve when they had an unexpected visitor. The Sun Dance was the biggest event in the Indians' round of life since the buffalo hunts were no more. Anyone and everyone attended. An unexpected visitor was an Indian named Calf Robe, who was wanted for horse stealing. The outlaw had come to the reserve believing that it was a place of sanctuary during their sacred rite of sun worship. Supt. Sam Steele, commanding Fort Macleod, believed otherwise.

Upon learning of Calf Robe's presence, Steele ordered Staff-Sgt. Chris Hilliard and two constables to go to the Blood camp near Stand-Off and arrest him. When Hilliard arrived he wasted no words and no time. Bursting into the Sun Dance lodge he placed Calf Robe under arrest and led him outside.

Outraged by this invasion of their sacred ceremony, the Indians became threatening. As the Mounties began to drag their captive to their horses they were encircled by more than 200 armed and menacing braves.

Steele later reported: "The men were often on the ground in their struggle with the Indians, and dozens of rifles were pointed at their heads as they lay on the ground hanging onto their prisoner, or when trying to bring him away, and at the last he was torn from them, and protected by over 200 howling braves, galloped off. It is a wonder there was no bloodshed and there most certainly would have been if the police had lost their heads and tried to draw their revolvers."

Steele was furious. He was determined to show the Indians that, Sun Dance or no Sun Dance, they could not treat the law with impunity.

The next day he ordered Inspector Winder and 20 men to go to the Blood camp and arrest Calf Robe and all the ringleaders of the resistance to the police. Realizing that it would be a very dangerous undertaking, he sent Potts along. About a mile outside the Blood reserve, the NWMP reined up and surveyed the lodges ahead. Potts suggested that it might be better if he rode into the camp alone and talked to Red Crow. Winder agreed.

Potts went straight to Red Crow's lodge. He told the chief that the NWMP had come for Calf Robe and they meant to have him. He also told him that the police wanted those who had helped him to escape. In the customary manner, the old chief sat down to smoke his pipe and think. Red Crow knew that Potts was not a bit fooled by the ruse, but he also knew that the half-blood, in his Indian way, would not pressure him for an immediate reply. The scout would return to the police with the chief's words then relay the Mountie's words. The old chief realized that Potts knew he was trying to extricate himself from the situation with his dignity intact.

Potts returned to Winder and explained what was taking place. Trusting his guide completely, Winder consented to play the game. He told Potts to tell Red Crow that he must have Calf Robe and "those who helped rescue him within one hour's time; and Red Crow must bring them in person. Otherwise we shall ride in and take them. In which case Red Crow will have to abide by the consequences."

The scout rode back into the Blood camp and went to Red Crow's lodge. This time he did not mince words. The chief knew Potts' reputation and standing was as great among the whites as it was among the Blackfoot. If the NWMP rode in Potts would be with them. With the time for talking over, Potts rode back to the police to wait.

(Left) A Mountie original, Sam Steele had a no-nonsense reputation with the force.
(Right) Head chief of the Bloods, Red Crow tried to bluff the Mounties into submission but found that they did not back down.

A long, tense hour passed. Just as Winder was giving the order to move into the camp, Red Crow appeared, leading Calf Robe and four other Indians. Again Potts' reputation and backwoods diplomacy had defused a potential powderkeg.

Winder took the five Bloods back to Fort Macleod where they were tried by Superintendent Steele and his inspectors. Steele was determined to have his pound of flesh. He sentenced Calf Robe and the others to jail terms, then severely chastised Red Crow for his part in the affair. But the Blood chief held fast to his belief that he had acted within the law in trying to protect his people and their sacred customs.

He would fight Steele's decision but do it in the whiteman's way—in the courts. Red Crow charged that the police had overstepped the bounds of their authority and used the whiteman's technicalities to fight his case. He argued that the arrests had been illegal since Steele, in his hot-headed way, had neglected to issue warrants for the arrest of Calf Robe and the others. The case became a cause celebre and the eastern newspapers blew it out of all proportion. Telegraph wires between Ottawa and Fort Macleod clicked continuously with messages and when the court finally ruled it found in Red Crow's favor: The arrests had been illegal.

The case was a milestone in the relationship between the Indians and whites. For those who wanted to see it was clear that the word of the NWMP given to the Blackfoot 15 years earlier was truth. There was only one law and it applied equally to red and white men—even to the police themselves. Potts was not one of those who had to wait so long to be convinced. He had long ago accepted the whiteman's system of justice. Later that year he went to Benton on police business and while in his old stomping grounds was told of a Blood Indian who was being held for horse stealing and was soon to be tried. The Indian did not speak English and Potts was asked to be his interpreter.

The trial was held on the night of January 14, 1890 and the next day the *Benton River Press* described the proceedings: "Under the glare of the electric light," the paper read, "Jerry, with his wrinkled front of thought, seemed an ancient Aztec come to judgement, and the Blood looked something like the last of the Mohicans lamenting the doom of his horse-stealing race."

The Indian was found guilty and also found not to be as ignorant of the English language as he pretended. As he was led away by the sheriff, he said slyly to Potts, "I ketch it."

When he returned to Fort Macleod, Potts found that Superintendent Steele had gone east on leave to be married; Commissioner Irvine was in the post on a tour of visit and inspection. One late winter's afternoon, as Irvine was lounging in boredom, Potts strolled up to him for some idle conversation. The Commissioner and Potts went back to the days when the NWMP had straggled, tired, hungry and lost into the Sweetgrass Hills and were led out by the ever-faithful scout.

They reminisced about those long ago days for a while and Potts told Irvine about his latest trip to Benton and his first encounter with electric lights. He wondered aloud if there might still not be some place where the buffalo still roamed and there was plenty of open space. Irvine sadly replied that there was not, and rambled on about how the country was settled, the land covered with farms and ranches instead of wandering Indians and buffalo. The country was linked from coast to coast by the longest railway in the world and they were stepping forward into the 20th century.

Potts thought a moment as he looked across the prairie, then, glancing at the commissioner, he said: "This country is getting too damn soft for me."

By no man's estimation could Potts be considered soft. He had not resisted the coming of the whiteman and his ways, but neither had he forsaken his Indian heritage. Like his Blackfoot brothers, he still craved the wild and free days but the softness he spoke of may have at last penetrated even his unassailable armor.

A year or so later Potts was duck hunting with a police constable named Tom Clarke when a flock suddenly rose from a slough and flew over Potts' head. Clarke blasted away. The Mountie got the fright of his life when the little scout tumbled to the ground. Running over, Clarke found Potts sitting in the reeds, rubbing his head. Relieved to find the scout alright he asked him what had happened.

"I thought somebody hit me in the head and knock my damn block off," Potts said, as he rubbed the side of his face. Clarke checked Potts for wounds and found that he was alright except for a single lead pellet that had lodged just beneath the skin behind his ear.

When they returned to the fort Potts, in his superstitious way, would not let the post surgeon remove the buckshot. He wanted to keep it as a good luck charm. Throughout his entire life, in all the fights and battles he had been in he had never once been touched by a bullet. The Blackfoot attributed this to Potts' supernatural powers, his medicine, but now they saw this occurrence as a bad omen. Potts, however, was amused by the fact that his only bullet wound had been received by accident at the hands of a friend, and a Mountie friend at that.

Soon he was making his newly acquired keepsake a topic of conversation and he never tired of telling the story of how he had come by it, especially when he was drinking. The story got to be a bore to the policemen at Fort Macleod. One night early in 1896, some Mounties were having a get together at the cabin of a man named John Clancey, and as always, invited Potts. One of the policemen decided that it was time to put an end to Potts' redundant yarn. When, as usual, the scout finished retelling the story for the *nth* time, the Mountie asked him to lean over so that they could all have a look. Eager to show off his good luck charm, Potts obliged.

Before he knew what was happening, the Mountie had flipped open his jackknife and surgically removed the pellet. In the morning when Potts unfogged his head and realized what had happened, he bemoaned the loss of his good luck charm and voiced his concern for the future.

Anyone not knowing Potts and listening to him probably grinned with amusement, but those who did know him and his unusual instincts probably felt a cold twinge of foreboding at his words.

Over the next few months Potts lived quietly, even sullenly. He continued to tend his horses and cattle and even seemed to enjoy himself as he organized and refereed horse races on the Piegan reserve. Yet he seemed to sense that his time was near. A son had been born to him recently and in the Indian tradition he had the boy brought to him to be named. Remembering a day long ago on the plains of Montana near Sun River and a fight with the Crows, he took the gun of blued steel that had almost killed him and bestowed it and the name of Blue Gun on his youngest child.

Soon afterwards, one day early in July, Potts began hemorrhaging from the lungs. He was taken to Fort Macleod where the post surgeon did all he could for him. But the chronic cough that had nagged him for the last decade or so, and his long bouts with the bottle had finally caught up with the tough, inscrutable Metis scout.

Potts lingered for a few days and, on July 14, 1896 he died. His death was officially recorded as due to consumption but one of his sons, who was 20 years old at the time, said that it was cancer of the throat aggravated by prolonged years of drinking. The man whose life perplexed so many confounded all even with his death.

The NWMP mourned the passing of their loyal, courageous and resourceful scout and interpreter and buried him with full military honors. Three volleys were fired over his resting place, each volley followed by a general salute. Potts was laid to rest in a small Roman Catholic cemetery east of the town of Fort Macleod which he had been instrumental in founding as the first white settlement in the Canadian northwest. A small, unimposing tombstone was inscribed with an epitaph that no doubt was in keeping with the way Potts would have wanted it, laconic.

> *In memory of Interpreter Jerry Potts*
> *D. Division. Died July 14, 1896*

The Fort Macleod *Gazette* of July 17, 1896 eulogized the passing of the Metis man: "Jerry Potts is dead. Through the whole Northwest, in many parts of Canada, and in England itself, this announcement will excite sorrow, in many cases sympathy, and in all interest. His memory will long live green in the hearts of those who knew him best, and 'faithful and true' is the character he leaves behind him—the best monument to a valuable life."

Of his value to the settling of the Canadian northwest there can be little doubt. Sam Steele, who worked with him as long as any whiteman and knew him as well as any man could, wrote: "It was a great pleasure to know Potts, for his conduct was always that of a gentleman, and he possessed most of the virtues and few of the faults of the races whose blood coursed through his veins. As an interpreter he was the most reliable that we ever had, truthful and clear . . . As a scout and guide I have never met his equal; he had none in either the north west or the states to the south. Many such men have been described in story and their feats related around many a camp fire, but none I have ever known or of whom I have read equalled him . . . It would take a large volume to describe even a small part of the usefulness of this man, his record being worthy of a place in the archives of the country which he served so well."

Jerry Potts is certainly worthy of a place in the archives of this country. Although he was not born here, he spent more than half his life in Canada and did it a service perhaps no other man of his day could have. He did it willingly, unselfishly, for no other reason than that he loved his people, the Blackfoot. He possessed the insight to know that the spread of white settlement could not be stopped. He was no less a Blackfoot for not fighting it, and no more a whiteman for accepting it.

Potts was truly a Renaissance man. He saw and understood and it was largely due to him that the history of the Canadian plains did not evolve as did that of the western United States, just a few miles south of the border. He was, "with his wrinkled front of thought . . . an ancient Aztec come to judgement"; perplexed perhaps by the ways of the whiteman but perceptive enought to recognize their inexorable destiny.

Jerry Potts is indeed an unsung hero. Perhaps that is as it should be, for that is the way he would have wanted it.